THE IDEA OF A PURE THEORY OF LAW

Most contemporary legal philosophers tend to take force to be an accessory to the law. According to this prevalent view the law primarily consists of a series of demands made on us; force, conversely, comes into play only when these demands fail to be satisfied. This book claims that this model should be jettisoned in favour of a radically different one: according to the proposed view, force is not an accessory to the law but rather its attribute. The law is not simply a set of rules incidentally guaranteed by force, but it should be understood as essentially rules about force.

The book explores in detail the nature of this claim and develops its corollaries. It then provides an overview of the contemporary jurisprudential debates relating to force and violence, and defends its claims against well-known counter-arguments by Hart, Raz and others.

This book offers an innovative insight into the concept of Pure Theory. In contrast to what was claimed by Hans Kelsen, the most eminent contributor to this theory, the author argues that the core insight of the Pure Theory is not to be found in the concept of a basic norm, or in the supposed absence of a conceptual relation between law and morality, but rather in the fundamental and comprehensive reformulation of how to model the functioning of the law intended as an ordering of force and violence.

The Idea of a Pure
Theory of Law

Christoph Kletzer

·HART·
PUBLISHING
OXFORD AND PORTLAND, OREGON
2018

Hart Publishing

An imprint of Bloomsbury Publishing Plc

Hart Publishing Ltd
Kemp House
Chawley Park
Cumnor Hill
Oxford OX2 9PH
UK

Bloomsbury Publishing Plc
50 Bedford Square
London
WC1B 3DP
UK

www.hartpub.co.uk
www.bloomsbury.com

Published in North America (US and Canada) by
Hart Publishing
c/o International Specialized Book Services
920 NE 58th Avenue, Suite 300
Portland, OR 97213-3786
USA

www.isbs.com

**HART PUBLISHING, the Hart/Stag logo, BLOOMSBURY and the
Diana logo are trademarks of Bloomsbury Publishing Plc**

First published 2018

British Library Cataloguing-in-Publication Data

A catalogue record for this book is available from the British Library.

ISBN: HB: 978-1-50991-343-5
       ePDF: 978-1-50991-345-9
       ePub: 978-1-50991-344-2

Library of Congress Cataloging-in-Publication Data

Names: Kletzer, Christoph, author.

Title: The idea of a pure theory of law / by Christoph Kletzer.

Description: Portland, Oregon : Hart Publishing, 2018. | Includes bibliographical references and index.

Identifiers: LCCN 2017048787 (print) | LCCN 2017052190 (ebook) | ISBN 9781509913442 (Epub) |
ISBN 9781509913435 (hardcover : alk. paper)

Subjects: LCSH: Law—Philosophy. | Jurisprudence. | Legal positivism.

Classification: LCC K339 (ebook) | LCC K339 .K54 2018 (print) | DDC 340/.1—dc23

LC record available at https://lccn.loc.gov/2017048787

Typeset by Compuscript Ltd, Shannon
Printed and bound in Great Britain by TJ International Ltd, Padstow, Cornwall

To find out more about our authors and books visit www.hartpublishing.co.uk. Here you will find extracts,
author information, details of forthcoming events and the option to sign up for our newsletters.

Contents

1

Introduction

IN THIS BOOK, I want to convince the reader that the law is an order of force or violence. I will also argue that this claim forms the doctrinal core of the Pure Theory of Law.

The book thus contains two sets of claims: a set of strong substantive claims and a set of weak exegetical ones. The strong claims take centre stage and come in the form of a theory of law which I try to clarify and present as being both defensible and superior to others. The weak claims are subsidiary and argue that this theory of law can be seen as comprising the core insight of the historical Pure Theory of Law.

This means that this book can fail or succeed on either both counts or on each count separately. Whilst I think that both the strong and weak, both the substantive and the exegetical, claims are inherently consistent and correct, the conjunction of both claims is by no means necessary and rests less on a necessary philosophical truth than on my desire to align myself with and contribute to the development of a tradition to which I feel I belong.

But what is the Pure Theory of Law? If we take the narrowest possible reading of the Pure Theory of Law, then it is limited to a couple of Hans Kelsen's writings; if we take the widest possible reading, then it is a theory that started with Fichte's philosophy of right, went through a neo-Kantian phase, reached its peak in the work of Hans Kelsen and his circle, was further developed and partly led astray by the Scandinavian Realists Ross and Olivecrona, was then carried forward into contemporary jurisprudence by the writing of Bobbio, Walter and Lippold, and is currently represented by, amongst others, authors like Paulson, Vinx, Jaestaedt, Jabloner, Somek and—I hope—me.

This book leans towards the wide reading of the Pure Theory of Law. It argues that behind all the different forms and shapes of theories that contribute to the historic Pure Theory of Law lies one idea: namely, that the law is an order of force or violence. That there is *one* idea behind these different forms and shapes of theories does not mean that the idea is a simple one. In this book, I try to introduce the complexity of this idea and defend it against criticism.

The exegetical claim thus provides the framework for the substantive claim. Whilst I put forward the strong substantive claim only because I believe it to be true, I put forward the exegetical claim also out of respect for and deference to a tradition. Leaving out the exegetical claim would be intellectually dishonest; after all, I am only picking up a theory which is already laid out *in nuce* in the many writings of the Pure Theory.

So, if someone convinced me that the ideas presented in this book are irreconcilable with the tradition of the Vienna School of Legal Positivism—which I think is impossible—then I would grudgingly let go of the label, would have to reconsider my intellectual journey and would look for a different heading under which to defend the theory presented herein. This brief elaboration of my intent is meant from the very outset to counter exegetical protestations of the kind: 'But on page 71 of the second edition of the Pure Theory Kelsen said something flatly contradicting your argument.' Of course he did. But Kelsen himself might be wrong about the Pure Theory—and he would have been the first to accept that.

According to the extra-wide reading on which I ground my elaborations, the Pure Theory started with the author who first used the tern 'Reine Rechtslehre' or 'Pure Theory of Law', namely, Johann Gottlieb Fichte.[1] Whilst allusions to some themes of the Pure Theory can already be found in Kant's separation of legality and morality, it was Fichte who radicalised and tidied up these Kantian arguments and tried to explicitly develop a theory of law as law, ie a theory of law separate from and independent of both moral philosophy and empirical knowledge, or a 'pure theory of law'. Fichte's theory was, understandably, couched in the language of Kantian natural law theory rather than in modern positivist lingo. Still, it laid out important claims familiar to a more contemporary rendering of the Pure Theory: Fichte argued that, despite not being reducible or dependent on moral argument, the law is nevertheless normative (semantic anti-reductionism), and he believed that knowledge of the law constituted a separate and distinctive field of human knowledge (purity). On top of that, he was the first to combine these theses with the fundamental insight, worked out in this book, that the law is an order of force or violence, and that permission plays a crucial role in understanding the distinctive normativity of the law.

The theoretical apex of the Pure Theory is found in the Vienna School of Legal Positivism, and within this school of thought Hans Kelsen's work without doubt deserves to be the main focus of attention. However, the fact that all the other thinkers and numerous contributors to the development of

---

[1] See JG Fichte, *Foundations of Natural Right*, ed F Neuhouser, trans M Baur (Cambridge, Cambridge University Press, 2000) 254. Baur translates the German term 'Reine Rechtslehre' as 'Pure doctrine of right' and not 'Pure theory of law'. This may be justified by the internal coherence of his translation and that fact that Baur, of course, did not have Kelsen in view.

the Pure Theory, such as Merkl, Verdross and Sander,[2] have received so little attention in the English-speaking academic world gives cause for some concern: not only do many of the doctrines attributed to Kelsen have their origin in the work of those authors, but Kelsen himself has throughout his life reconsidered or even overthrown his ideas in the light of criticism and the discourse he has been engaged in. It would be hard to see any logic to these developments if one does not consider them all to be attempts to further a project somehow independent of the various historic renderings, namely the project of finding a coherent formulation of a Pure Theory of Law. This project, in turn, can only be understood in its significance as a collective project and not as the monomaniacal *idée fixe* of a single individual. The crux of the project is the following: how can we establish and deliver a knowledge of law as law, ie a knowledge of the law as not being a department of morality, metaphysics or the empirical social sciences? How would we have to conceive of the law for this kind of knowledge to be possible? As will be developed in this book, what came to the fore in these questions was that for such a knowledge to be possible we would have to understand the law as an order of force. I will outline the nature of the specific question of the Pure Theory and why I believe it has to be put in this specific way in the next chapter.

The idea that the law is fundamentally an order of force or violence was first made fully explicit by the Scandinavian realists, predominantly Olivecrona and Ross. In their attempt to isolate this point, however, they were led to believe that they had to jettison one of the core ideas of the Pure Theory, namely that the law is actually law and thus normative.

That discarding normativity is by no means necessary has been shown by Norberto Bobbio: we can understand that the law as an order of force without letting go of the normativity of the law. Similar claims have been forwarded by Paulson. In this book, I pick up these threads and try to develop them further.

This idea of the law as an order of force has merged somewhat into the background, if not completely vanished, in most contemporary treatments of the Pure Theory. In Vinx's important contribution *Hans Kelsen's Pure Theory of Law*,[3] for instance, force or violence hardly takes centre stage. I am not claiming that this makes Vinx's contribution worth any less. As an introduction and defence of *Kelsen's* Pure Theory of Law, his book is certainly of central

---

[2] Unfortunately, little of the work is available in English. For a good overview of the thinkers contributing to the Vienna School of Legal Positivism or associated with it, see R Walter et al (eds), *Der Kreis um Hans Kelsen. Die Anfangsjahre der Reinen Rechtslehre* (Vienna, Manz, 2008); for a volume bringing together the writings of Kelsen, Merkl and Verdross, see HR Klecatsky et al (eds), *Die Wiener rechtstheoretische Schule. Schriften von Hans Kelsen, Adolf Merkl, Alfred Verdross* (Vienna, Verlag Österreich, 2010).

[3] L Vinx, *Kelsen's Pure Theory of Law. Legality and Legitimacy* (Oxford, Oxford University Press, 2007).

importance and very instructive. Like most others, however, it stops just short of fully following through on the trajectory outlined.

I try to remedy this omission herein. This book thus does not aim to give a comprehensive rendering of the Pure Theory. This has been done very well by Kelsen himself, and, in addition to Vinx, by authors such as Walter[4] or Lippold.[5] In this book I want to highlight what has been left open in these renderings and what I think is nevertheless central to the understanding of the Pure Theory, since it forms the missing keystone of the theoretical arch of the Pure Theory. Only with this keystone can the other claims be rendered structurally sound.

As already mentioned, the book does not only, or even primarily, address this tradition; rather, it aims to convince everyone that the law actually is an order of force or violence. As such, it engages more with common sense, as portrayed by Hart and Raz, than with Sander, Vinx or Lippold. One certainly does not need to be a seasoned expert in the literature of the Pure Theory in order to be able to appreciate the arguments presented in this book.

In what follows, I will first (in chapter two) outline the project of the Pure Theory, and set out what kind of a theory the Pure Theory aims to be and what it can at best hope to be. Then, in the three chapters following this preliminary outline, I will present the core of the argument. In chapter three, I will introduce the main idea of the book, namely that the law is an order of violence. This will not only require careful arguments that aim to refute classical jurisprudential challenges to a claim of this kind, but will also require something both more subtle and more ambitious: a change of perspective or standpoint in relation to the law. I try to facilitate this change of perspective by giving examples, partly taken from ancient Roman law. In chapter four, I focus on the concept of permission, which, I argue, is necessary to understand the specific normativity of the law. Finally, in chapter five, I will introduce how, according to the Pure Theory, the law does all of that, namely, by means of functioning as a schema of interpretation.

After discussing the core of what I take to be the main contribution of the Pure Theory, the next two chapters deal with two important repercussions of this core doctrine. The first, discussed in chapter six, deals with the relation between law and morality. The argument presented is that law cannot have any relation to morality as both cannot be considered to be valid simultaneously. The second, developed in chapter seven, tries to locate the Pure Theory within the contemporary discussion of positivism and argues that the Pure Theory presents an attempt to formulate a theory of what could be called 'absolute positivism'.

---

[4] R Walter, *Der Aufbau der Rechtsordnung* (Vienna, Manz, 1974).
[5] R Lippold, *Recht und Ordnung. Statik und Dynamik der Rechtsordnung* (Vienna, Manz, 2000).

2

The Purity of the Pure Theory of Law

I. WHAT IS THE PURE THEORY OF LAW?

The content of the Pure Theory narrowly understood can be presented in terms of six canonical doctrines:

1. The doctrine of normativity (semantic anti-reductionism).[1]
2. The doctrine of the double purity of legal theory.[2]
3. The doctrine of the basic norm.[3]
4. The doctrine of the complete legal norm.[4]
5. The doctrine of the hierarchical structure of the legal system.[5]
6. The doctrine of alternative authorisation.[6]

I would certainly count anybody who subscribes to all or nearly all of these doctrines as a proponent of the Pure Theory of Law.

This book, however, is not directly concerned with these doctrines. In my view, these doctrines make up the vast periphery of the Pure Theory. I call them peripheral not because they are irrelevant, but because they all radiate from a core or centre. This centre of the Pure Theory can be put most succinctly in the following claim:

— The law is an order of force or violence.[7]

---

[1] Roughly, the claim that law actually is normative and that it is not explicable in factual terms only.

[2] The claim that in studying the law we have to make sure that we keep the law strictly separate from both morality and sociology.

[3] The claim that in referring to the law we have always already presupposed the basic norm.

[4] The claim that the only norm that is complete is the one that gives all conditions of the lawfulness of an act of force.

[5] The claim that the content of the law is created dynamically by a series of legal acts progressively individuating the conditions of the lawfulness of the use of force.

[6] The doctrine that, in authorising the annulment of certain laws, the law has thereby stipulated the (provisional) legality of unlawful law.

[7] In this book, the terms 'violence' and 'force' are used more or less interchangeably. My use of both words is meant to convey the sense of the Latin term *vis*, which, whilst considered to be closer to force than to violence, still carries the connotation of the latter: '*Vis* was a neutral concept, nearer to our "force" than "violence", so there was no difficulty in applying it to both illegal violence and legal self-help' (AW Lintott, *Violence in Republican Rome* (Oxford, Clarendon, 1968) 22–23).

On the one hand, this is a claim that can be either true or false—and I will argue that it is true. On the other hand, it is more than that: it represents a standpoint in relation to the law that is in competition with other jurisprudential standpoints. As a standpoint, it exhibits a certain internal complexity. This internal complexity consists not only in a loose series of supposedly true statements, but also in an integrated view of the law. This view can be outlined as follows:

— The law is a normative formation that orders society by permitting the use of force or violence by means of schematising the interpretation of force or violence.

The Pure Theory thus consists of cascading claims of derivations leading us from the surface to the more basic or primitive operations of the law. The argument runs through the following stages: on the surface level, the law regulates society by creating obligations. But how does the law create obligations? It does so by regulating force or violence. How does it regulate force? By permitting the use of force. How does it permit force? By schematising interpretations.

This is roughly what I will be arguing and defending in this book. Before doing that, however, I want to clarify the nature and status of the claims made in the book. Those not interested in such a clarification of what kind of a theory the Pure Theory of Law is can skip immediately to the next chapter.

II. THE CONTEST OF STANDPOINTS

As mentioned above, the Pure Theory of Law is more than just a series of statements that claim to be true. Rather, it presents a standpoint in relation to the law, a certain view of the law. This standpoint and the view it offers are fundamentally different from the standpoint and view usually taken. The Pure Theory claims that its standpoint is superior to the one commonly taken and thus invites us or requires us to change our point of view.

To claim superiority over another standpoint does not mean to claim that one's arguments are straightforwardly right and the other's are simply wrong. It is unlikely that in philosophy anybody's position is simply wrong about anything. The conviction that someone is simply wrong is often indicative less of the weakness of the attacked position and more of the incompleteness of one's engagement with it.

If the claim of superiority does not mean that another position is simply refuted, what does it mean? It is less mysterious than it might sound: in order to demonstrate that a standpoint is superior to another, all one needs to show is that the other standpoint is encompassed by the standpoint presented as superior, but not the other way around. So, in order to demonstrate the superiority of a standpoint, one needs to demonstrate that, by taking this standpoint, one can see everything that can be seen from the other standpoint, but not vice versa. The superior standpoint thus has in view both everything that the other standpoint sees *and also* the other standpoint itself. Thus, the superior standpoint can not only explain how the intellectual terrain is actually laid out, but also why, viewed from an inferior standpoint, it appears the way it does.

What characterises the relation of the higher standpoint to the lower is *explanatory primacy*: the higher standpoint gives a better explanation than the lower because it explains everything the lower standpoint does and also explains things the lower standpoint cannot explain. What characterises the relation of the lower standpoint to the higher is *superfluity*: given the higher standpoint, the lower one becomes superfluous. Throughout the book I will thus keep referring not only to the wrongness of alternative claims, but also to their superfluity, and I will refer not only to the rightness of the Pure Theory, but also to its explanatory primacy.

Of course, I will be arguing that one should take the standpoint that the law is a comprehensive order of violence or force because the law actually is such a comprehensive order. However, I will also offer the weaker claim that the Pure Theory presents a higher standpoint in relation to competing theories, such as that the law is a union of primary and secondary norms, a set of orders backed up by a threat of sanction, or the morally most appealing interpretation of the rules that allow for the use of violence or a comprehensive, supreme and open institutional normative system.

III. THE KANTIAN MANOEUVRE

The author who was the first to explicitly make use of such a standpoint claim was Kant. He did not claim that rival philosophical positions, like empiricism or dogmatism, were simply wrong. This would have been an unpromising strategy: proving something wrong requires some external standard, and it is hard to see what could play the role of such an external standard for a comprehensive philosophical worldview—especially as empiricism and dogmatism both seem internally consistent.

So Kant had to take a detour: he did not argue that empiricism and dogmatism are wrong by any external standard, but that holding them comes at too high a theoretical cost. He argued that one cannot be committed to empiricism and at the same time make sense of our knowledge of the external world. The same is true for dogmatism. So, whilst Kant does not directly demonstrate the falsity of empiricism or dogmatism, he demonstrates that we cannot hold them *and* have a working theory of knowledge. We just cannot have it all.

This move was necessary in order to demonstrate that his own theory, transcendental idealism,[8] which at first is highly implausible, if not offensive to common sense, is not only a contender to philosophical truth, but ends up as the only route left open. The result of this long journey is not simply that transcendental realism is false and that transcendental idealism is true, but rather that transcendental idealism presents the higher standpoint in relation to transcendental realism. It explains everything that we hoped transcendental realism can explain, it explains things which cannot be explained from the inferior standpoint and it explains why the inferior standpoint falls for the illusions in the way it does. For common sense, it might at first be a real struggle to reach this higher standpoint, but it turns out that, judged by common sense's own standards, it is worth it.

A similar constellation of common sense, intellectual costs and philosophical truth can be found in the emblematic example Kant used to rely on, the Copernican revolution: one can of course describe the movement of the celestial objects starting from and in line with what we immediately perceive and with what seems right to common sense, namely that the earth is fixed and the sun moves around the earth, but this comes at a very high theoretical cost: we have to introduce pseudo-forces to explain the odd paths drawn on the sky. Pseudo-forces as such are not necessarily anathema in physics. We often use them to make sense of mechanical systems. The centrifugal force, for instance, is such a pseudo-force, yet we have no qualms about referring to it. So it is not primarily that the common-sense standpoint is simply wrong or incoherent that pushes us to leave it behind, it is that we can avoid the costs that come with it. As soon as we leave the comfortable zone of our common-sense views and posit something seemingly absurd, namely that the earth moves around the sun, we see how things suddenly all fall into place. Whilst common sense might have first rebelled against moving in the direction of the higher standpoint, in the end it finds fuller satisfaction there.

The Pure Theory requires a similar jettisoning of some tacit common-sense convictions. That such a discomfort is worthwhile, however, can only be established by demonstrating that the Pure Theory does indeed deliver the higher standpoint it promises.

Thus, the Pure Theory, just like Kant's criticism or the Copernican manoeuvre, does not require a complete suspension of common sense. It would be hard to know what should guide us if we were to completely discard common sense. The Pure Theory requires merely the willingness to partially and temporarily suspend a certain satisfaction we find in common sense in

---

[8] I roughly follow Henry Allison's take on transcendental idealism. See H Allison, *Kant's Transcendental Idealism: An Interpretation and Defence* (New Haven, Yale University Press, 1983).

order to reach a firmer and deeper satisfaction in the end. The Pure Theory turns common sense against itself.

There is another, related, sense in which the Pure Theory is a deeply Kantian project: it takes seriously the difficulty of reaching a truly human understanding of the law, or an understanding of the law *as* law. This must sound odd. Does not every contemporary jurisprudential school, apart maybe from avowedly theological schools of natural law, succeed in at least describing law as human all the way down?

This has to be doubted. To see why, let me again outline a Kantian dilemma first and then show how the Pure Theory struggles with similar themes: Kant argued that, unbeknownst to ourselves, in our everyday model of knowledge we essentially rely on the idea of god as a regulative idea. Henry Allison put it as follows:

> By such a theocentric model I understand a programme or method of epistemological reflection, according to which human knowledge is analysed and evaluated in terms of its conformity, or lack thereof, to the standard of cognition theoretically achievable by an 'absolute' or 'infinite intellect'. By the latter I understand one that is not encumbered by the limitations of the human intellect, and which, therefore, knows objects 'as they are in themselves'. Such an intellect functions in this model essentially as a regulative idea in the Kantian sense. Thus the appeal to it does not commit one either to the existence of such an intellect or to the assumption that knowledge of this type is actually possessed by the human mind. The point is only that a hypothetical 'God's-eye view' of things is used as a standard in terms of which the 'objectivity' of human knowledge is analysed.[9]

According to our common-sense model of knowledge, our representations of the world are true if and only if they correspond with the things as they are out there in the world independently of our representation of them. It is hard for us to even conceive of an alternative model of truth and knowledge. However, the problem with such a model is that only an absolute intellect has access to the things as they are in themselves, independently of our apperception. Thus, we can never compare our representations with how things really are in themselves. Still, if we hold on to our everyday notion of knowledge, we have to deem such a comparison possible. In our ordinary, everyday model of knowledge, be it a thoroughly empiricist or naturalistic one, we thus implicitly refer to a divine point of view—a point of view, however, which we can never inhabit. Sceptical arguments, which flatly deny the possibility of any knowledge, rest their plausibility precisely on this differential between a divine and a human point of view. A successful refutation of the sceptic thus does not consist in the demonstration of a flaw in his argument, but in the rejection of the standards of true knowledge that he presupposes.

---

[9] ibid 19.

So, in his *Critique of Pure Reason*, Kant tries to develop a theory of knowledge purely from the human point of view, ie a theory of knowledge which at no point makes reference to a divine point of view. The major task of such a theory consists in reinterpreting the object of knowledge from the thing itself to a phenomenal object of cognition so that 'the cognitive structure of the human mind is viewed as the source of certain conditions which must be met by anything that is to be represented as an object by such a mind'.[10]

Why is this relevant? It shows us that it is harder than one might have thought to reach a truly and fully human way of making sense of knowledge, ie a way that does not implicitly or latently refer to contentious theological or metaphysical ideas. We might believe that we have left the theological world-view behind, that our concepts are completely naturalistic, but, as Kant has shown, in our very concept of knowledge we might still be implicitly but deeply wedded to metaphysical and theological commitments. According to Kant, the project of enlightenment is thus still incomplete and ongoing. It is certainly not reached in common sense or scientific empiricism, as this carries with it a metaphysical birth defect. In order to complete enlightenment, to complete the anthropocentric turn, in order to make sense of knowledge as not metaphysically problematic, we might have to completely reconstruct our model of knowledge. This project is still ongoing.

In a similar sense, the Pure Theory of Law can be understood as a project, still ongoing, that tries to find a way of understanding the law as fully human. What distinguishes the Pure Theory in this respect from most other jurisprudential theories is that it finds a philosophical problem where others do not. The Pure Theory is an attempt to deal with this problem, to crack this nut.

This whole constellation of questions points to a particular difficulty of legal philosophy in the modern age: whilst we Moderns have largely thrown out and rescinded all formerly valid forms of metaphysical and theological legitimation, our conceptual universe is still awash with the remnants of these modes of legitimation and our conceptual repertoire is still pregnant with them. Many of our concepts (validity, obligation, duty, etc) have been born as responses to originally metaphysical questions; they are vessels which were originally meant to be filled with metaphysical or theological content.[11] Now that this content has become unavailable, the adequacy of this entire conceptual universe is put into question.

The Pure Theory of Law is a theory that tries to take up this challenge and tries to answer how positive law qua positive law, ie a law which is fully human

---

[10] ibid 29.

[11] Anscombe famously advised that we should completely stop using these concepts, to jettison them until we have cleared up the groundwork. GEM Anscombe, 'Modern Moral Philosophy' (1958) 33 *Philosophy* 1, 1.

and does not rely on theological or otherwise metaphysical presuppositions, could be possible at all. The question of the Pure Theory thus becomes: 'How is human law possible?' or, more precisely: 'How do we have to conceptualise the nature of positive law so that it is possible as secular or truly human law?' What unifies the various authors I have mentioned in the introduction, from Fichte to Paulson, is their struggle in this common quest.

IV. THE PURITY OF THE PURE THEORY

This fundamentally Kantian question provides, I think, the key to understanding the purity of the Pure Theory. The demand of purity is not based in some arbitrary, maybe fetishist, desire for formality, tidiness or austerity,[12] but results as a requirement of answering the much deeper question, introduced above: 'How is human law possible?'

In order for law to be law, it has to be normative, ie it has to create obligations. Otherwise it would not be law. This might at first seem a merely stipulative claim: after all, could it not be the case that the law does not create obligations, ie that there is no such law at all in existence which is capable of creating obligations? Yes, of course this would be possible. But this result would only be problematic for the project of the Pure Theory if its project were answering the question: 'What is the true concept of law and does such a concept include true obligation?' If this were our question, then of course a stipulation would be a lazy cop-out. But this is not our question. Our question is: 'If we are to conceive of a law that created true obligations, how would it have to be constructed and how would we have to conceive of our approach to it for it to be possible?' So the Pure Theory does not ask what is the concept of law, but rather how is law of a specific quality possible?

Given this question and given that we want to answer it without reference to metaphysically contentious claims, ie given that we want to understand law as fully human, the nature of this obligation has to be explained entirely from the law itself. We have thus reached the conventional conception of purity: the Pure Theory embraces semantic non-reductivism, ie it takes the law to create obligations and at the same time it has to remain 'free of sociological and psychological investigations and it has to separate law from morality'.[13]

This contemporary way of describing purity, however, makes it sound as if it were the spleen of an author. It does not explain why purity is needed or what function it serves. As I hope I have already hinted, the purity of the Pure

---

[12] J Raz, 'The Purity of the Pure Theory' in S Paulson (ed), *Normativity and Norms: Critical Perspectives on Kelsenian Themes* (Oxford, Oxford University Press, 1998) 237.
[13] ibid.

Theory is rather a result of reflections of the relationship between law and knowledge.

It is a virtue, if not a pre-condition, of a philosophical position to not only present reasonable claims about its object (god, the world, mind, the law), but to also make explicit the conditions under which the relation to the specific object can be possible and successful. After all, since the crux of a philosophical problem is very often hidden in plain sight, a philosophical position should not shy away from constantly assuring itself of whether the assumed relation to the object is possible at all. So, in a sense, if one wants to answer the questions, say, 'What is matter?' and 'What is mind?' in a philosophical way it is not enough to present a list of well-reasoned statements about the nature or essence of mind or matter, eg 'matter is infinitely divisible' or 'mind is an illusion', but it is necessary to inquire whether and how we, as philosophers, can relate to these objects at all. After all, it might turn out that the answers we have reached lead to an understanding of the object which, if taken seriously, makes it impossible for us to relate to the object in question. However, if we cannot make sense of our relation to the object, then we cannot make sense of our knowledge of it and then our knowledge turns into nonsense.

Philosophy is thus always a reflexive enterprise: while trying to make sense of an object, we also have to make sense of our possibility to relate to that object. The Pure Theory is an avowedly reflexive philosophy of law. I thus think it is one of the few truly philosophical approaches to the law.

In this book, I will at many stages contrast what I take to be the philosophical standpoint of the Pure Theory, according to which the law is at its core an order of force or violence, with the common jurisprudential standpoint, according to which the law at its core is a system of demands, requests or mandatory norms. This contrast will take many forms and will also be given a series of different labels. In the next section, I will briefly lay out what I take this common-sense demand model of the law to entail.

V. THE PRIMITIVE FUNCTION OF THE LAW

The law cannot by and of itself immediately bring about states of affairs. It cannot by itself alleviate social ills, build roads, distribute wealth, secure health services or imprison people. After all, the law is, in a sense, language. So if the law somehow does all of these things, how does it do them?

One common view is that at its most basic level the law functions by telling people what to do. According to this view, the law basically hands out orders, issues norms, sets standards, gives reasons for action and makes courses of action mandatory. Understood this way, the pragmatics of the law are similar to the pragmatics of morality: first, an ideal state of affairs is set out; then the actual world is compared with this state of affairs; next, the actual world is found to be deficient; and finally it is told to be more like the ideal state of affairs and less like it actually is. Understood this way, the law is a demand made on the world, mainly on human agents within this world. This demand can present itself as a standard, a command, an ought or a norm.

In what follows, I will present some principled problems with this demand view. In the rest of the book, I will try to defend the claim of the Pure Theory that there is a better way of understanding the basic operation of the law. According to the Pure Theory, the law operates at the null level not by telling people what to do, not by making demands, but by schematising the interpretation of the use of force or violence as lawful and thus permitted. The argument presented is thus not that the law does not make demands, but rather that *at the basic level* it does not make demands but schematises interpretations. In so far as the law does indeed issue demands, it does so by means of schematising interpretations in the way described in this book. What the Pure Theory thus does is not to straightforwardly refute the demand view of the law, but to claim that the view presented here has explanatory primacy and that the demand view is thus superfluous.

In arguing in favour of one basic model of the functioning of the law against another, I am assuming that there is such a basic model. By such a primitive function, I refer to a model of the basic pragmatic operations of the law in terms of which the more complex operations of the law are effected and in turn explained. But one might be tempted to deny that such a primitive function exists at all.

One could, instead, claim that the law simply lacks a single function in terms of which the other functions can be explained, that it rests on an irreducible multiplicity, that it is not based on a common core but a rhizomatic plurality.

At least at some passages Hart seems to argue just that. However, even Hart, who is explicitly trying to resist the 'strong itch for uniformity in jurisprudence',[14] who tries not to artificially flatten the variety of laws, is himself committed to a primitive function of the law.

Let us briefly follow Hart's claim. He argues: (i) that there are a variety of laws and that 'surely not all laws order people to do or not to do things';[15] (ii) that any promising attempt to reduce apparently distinct varieties of legal rule to a single form alleged to convey the quintessence of law make the sanction a centrally important element, and both will 'fail if it is shown that law without sanction is perfectly conceivable';[16] and (iii) that reducing the variety of laws to

---

[14] HLA Hart, *The Concept of Law*, 2nd edn (Oxford, Oxford University Press, 1994) 32.
[15] ibid 26.
[16] ibid 38.

a single type can only be 'purchased ... at too high a price: that of distorting the different social functions which different types of rules perform'.[17]

Let us look at these claims in turn. The first claim (i) is either trivially true or is begging the question: of course no one would deny that there are a variety of laws. The question is whether these various laws can be explained, whether their functioning can be enlightened in terms of a more primitive, unitary functioning of the law. Note that to claim that the variety of laws can be explained in terms of some primitive function does not mean that the variety is reducible to this primitive function.[18] To claim that the functioning of my body can be explained by referring to its organs does not commit one to claiming that the functioning of the whole body can be reduced to the functioning of the separate components. Rather, it is the specific assemblage of these organs that makes the body as a whole work. So the fact that some laws order people to do things and others confer powers does not contradict the claim that there is a primitive function as long as one law can be explained in terms of another or both can be explained in terms of a third kind of law. It is thus irrelevant whether or not 'all laws order people to do things or not to do things'—actually, the Pure Theory claims, all laws can be better understood in terms of laws that do *not* order people to do or not to do things.

The second claim (ii), conversely, is either wrong or beside the point. First, it is simply not the case that any promising attempt to reduce apparently distinct varieties of legal rule to a single form has to make the sanction a central element. The Pure Theory as introduced in this book is an example of such a theory that explains distinct varieties of legal rule in terms of a single form without referring to sanction. Secondly, as will be argued in detail in chapter three, whilst it is indeed the case that 'law without sanction is perfectly conceivable', it is not the case that law without force or violence is perfectly conceivable.

The third claim (iii) returns to what has been left open by the first: does a theory of a primitive function of the law necessarily commit one to 'distorting the different social functions which different types of rules perform'? Well, not really. Let us look more closely: the fact that different social functions are performed does not mean that these social functions cannot be explained in terms of one and the same primitive function. To take an anatomical analogy: the heart and the iris sphincter perform different functions. However, it would be wrong to allow this difference in function to bar us from noting that both the heart and the iris sphincter operate by muscular contraction. Also, I do not think that Hart would deny that the law prohibiting assault and the law

---

[17] ibid 38.
[18] This is often overlooked. See, eg, A Marmor, *Philosophy of Law* (Princeton, Princeton University Press, 2011) 39–40.

demanding damages for tortious behaviour perform different social functions. Yet, Hart would himself claim that each performs its social function by means of duty-imposing rules. So, Hart himself is not really committed to the claim that a difference in function can only be effected by different kinds of rules. He is only committed to this claim when directed against someone else. In the case of explaining the different functions (criminal and tort law) in terms of the same rules (duty imposing rules), Hart seems less troubled that this would be performing a harmful distortion. It thus seems that Hart simply applies a different level of explanatory granularity. For him, on the face of it, there are two kinds of rules: duty-imposing duties and power-conferring rules.

Or are there? After all, on closer look, Hart reveals that he himself at least toys with a primitive function of the law, namely, that the law basically sets standards. In one passage, he concedes that the two basic kinds of laws—the power-conferring rules and the duty-imposing rules—both 'constitute *standards* by which particular actions may be thus critically appraised. So much is perhaps implied in speaking of them both as rules.'[19]

This standard-setting function of the law is certainly the key to Hart's understanding.

> The principal functions of the law as a means of social control are not to be seen in private litigation or prosecutions, which represent vital but still ancillary provisions for the failures of the system. It is to be seen in the diverse ways in which the law is used to control, to guide, and to plan life out of court.[20]

This standard setting function is thus, according to Hart, effected by rules. 'The ideas of orders, obedience, habits and threats, do not include, and cannot by their combination yield, the idea of a rule, without which we cannot hope to elucidate even the most elementary forms of law'.[21]

Hart thus ends up with a primitive function of the law. In the end, it would be hard to see what the philosophical value added would be if we did not achieve at least some kind of explanatory unification. A philosophical treatment of law cannot be content to simply restate the legal material; rather, it needs to comprehend it philosophically, ie it needs to 'come to terms' with it. Ultimately, it is as if Hart is arguing against the Pure Theory along the following lines: you are not only wrong in your solution, but you are doubly wrong because the problem for which you are trying to find a solution is a pseudo-problem and does not have a solution—now here my own solution to this problem …!

[19] Hart (n 14) 33. Original emphasis.
[20] ibid 40.
[21] ibid 80.

VI. THE DEMAND MODEL OF THE FUNCTIONING OF LAW

We have now seen that Hart, despite some early protestations to the contrary, endorses a singular model of the primitive function of the law. This model is what we have above called the demand model. Most contemporary juris-prudes, Hartian, Razian or neither, work under this model. This cannot be surprising. What, after all, should the law do apart from telling us what to do?

In this book, I will repeatedly try to show the inadequacy of this demand model. I will claim that at the basic level the law does not tell us what to do, but it does permit the use of force. Here, I will outline a couple of principled and interlaced difficulties with the demand model which militate in favour of discarding it altogether. I actually think that the various reasons against the demand model listed below are all variants of one and the same aporia into which the demand model invariably leads us. I will not, however, pursue such a strong claim here. Instead, I am content to present some familiar difficul-ties of the demand model that should suffice to convince the reader that it is worthwhile to at least consider the Pure Theory as an alternative.

(i) The demand model mainly assumes that legal norms function in a way similar to moral norms. It thus tends to tie up the law with reasons-talk: it takes legal norms to provide or aim to provide reasons for action. However, it is an open question whether this has to be the case. Kramer and MacCormick, for instance, have rightly noted that if we consider the law as consisting not of prescriptions but of commands, then the necessity and attractiveness of the reasons-talk immediately vanishes. Commands, after all, do 'not necessar-ily lay down or presuppose reasons-for-action for their addressees'.[22] Rather, they are based in an actual superiority of the issuer of the imperative over the addressee of the imperative. I am not arguing that Kramer is right on that. All that needs to be noted is that the demand model simply assumes that jurisprudence has to engage in reasons-talk by understanding legal norms as prescriptions. The philosophical question, however, is how legal norms should be understood in the first place. A stipulation will not do. The Pure Theory, as introduced and defended in this book, presents an alternative to the demand model and a refinement of the institutionalist model offered by MacCormick: it is neither the case that the law at the base level aims to give (moral) reasons to its subjects nor that the law requires an existing institution of centralised state-coercion to guarantee the superiority needed for the possibility of issuing imperatives. Rather, the law at the basic level simply allows the use of force. By this permission of force, the law at the same time both provides a structure of

---

[22] M Kramer, *In Defence of Legal Positivism. Law Without Trimmings* (Oxford, Oxford University Press, 1999) 84.

prudential reasons for action and constitutes (ie, it does not merely rely on) the superiority of the state, thus allowing it to issue certain commands.

(ii) But even if we accepted that reason-talk was necessary to understand the law, it is unclear how exactly the law qua law can give reasons. There remains a stubborn is/ought gap between the fact that someone utters some words and the situation of me actually having a truly new reason—or, for that matter, an obligation—to do something. That I ought to do something seems to require some other normative fact. This normative fact might be hidden, but it has to be there. So the situation has to appear as follows: the law as law cannot give us new reasons or obligations at all; in so far as it seems the case that it does give us reasons, then it is something else that is ultimately responsible for giving us the respective reasons or obligations. Much jurisprudential energy has been expended fogging this issue. It is thus no surprise that at some point it emerged that all the law can do is trigger pre-existent genuine reasons.[23]

(iii) The demand model, ie the view that the law works by telling us what to do, ultimately rests on the assumption that it is a good thing to have the law. But this needs to be doubted. Of course, if it is a good thing to have law and if the law consists in trying to tell us what to do, then the law might be in a good position to succeed in telling us what to do. But is it good to have law? It is, of course, a good thing to have good law, but since not all law is perforce good law, the litmus test for the demand model is this: is it also a good thing to have non-good law?[24] This is a highly contentious issue and resting one's basic philosophical commitment on such a delicate issue is theoretically quite risky. I think it would be wise to have an understanding of law that can make sense of the law even if it is not necessarily the case that it is a good thing to have bad law.

There is one strategy that is regularly reverted to in order to insulate the demand model against criticism like the above. This strategy comes in many forms, but since Gardner's is the most accessible and, I think, most succinct, I will discuss his *pars pro toto*: Gardner tries to deflate the dependence of the

---

[23] D Enoch, 'Giving Practical Reasons' (2011) 11 *The Philosopher's Imprint* 1; D Enoch, 'Reason-Giving and the Law' in L Green et al (eds), *Oxford Studies in the Philosophy of Law, vol 1* (Oxford, Oxford University Press, 2011) 1–38. Critical KM Ehrenberg, *The Functions of Law* (Oxford, Oxford University Press, 2016) 155; V Rodriguez-Blanco, 'Reasons in Action v Triggering Reasons: A Reply to Enoch on Reason-Giving and Legal Normativity' [2013] *Problema* 7, biblio.juridicas.unam.mx/revista/Filoso aDerecho.

[24] Nigel Simmonds has forcefully argued that it is and Matthew Kramer has argued against him. See N Simmonds, 'Straightforwardly False: The Collapse of Kramer's Positivism' (2004) 63 *CLJ* 98; N Simmonds, 'Freedom, Law, and Naked Violence: A Reply to Kramer' (2009) 59 *The University of Toronto Law Journal* 381; M Kramer, 'On the Moral Status of the Rule of Law' (2004) 63 *CLJ* 65. See also NJ McBride and S Steel, *Great Debates in Jurisprudence* (London, Palgrave Macmillan 2014) 76.

reasons (and obligations) given by the law from the reasons to have law in the first place. He argues that the former are independent of the latter. An argument to that effect would indeed be strictly necessary for the demand model to make sense. I will try to show, however, that it fails.

Gardner argues that an authoritative norm might 'make it right, by its demands, to do what would otherwise be wrong'.[25] If we have a reason or duty to support an institution, we might have a reason or duty to do what that institution demands from us and this reason or duty is different and distinguishable from what duties we have independently from this institution, and thus also different and distinguishable from the reasons to enter the institution in the first place:

> Many moral reasons share the following structure: being a friend is a reason for acts of friendship, being a judge is a reason for judicial acts, being a citizen is a reason to do one's citizenly duty, etc. These reasons may appear to lift themselves by their own bootstraps. But of course they do not quite do so. They presuppose that one may have a reason for being someone's friend, or for being a judge, or for being a citizen. But that reason may be something quite modest. One has a reason to make friends with someone just in case, for example, one enjoys their company. One has reason to be a judge just in case it would be a good career move. One has reason to become a citizen just in case this will allow one to escape persecution elsewhere. This need not be a moral reason. Nor need it be a reason to perform, separately, any of the particular acts which, as a friend or as a judge or a citizen, one must then go on to perform. These further acts are made rational, and indeed in some cases morally required, by the fact that one is a friend or a judge, not by the reason one had to become a friend or a judge in the first place.[26]

I do not think that this is right. But before trying to show where Gardner goes wrong, let us consider why he has to go down this route in the first place. For Gardner's entire argument that an authoritative norm might 'make it right, by its demands, to do what would otherwise be wrong' to work, he needs to show not only that it is reasonable to follow a demand issued by an authority, but also that this reasonability does not in turn simply depend on or is contained in the reasons for entering the institution from where the demands ensue. He thus needs to make sure he can establish that the reasons provided by an institution for doing x, the institutional reasons i, are logically independent from the reasons for entering an institution, the entry reasons e. If he can show this to be the case, he believes, then he has demonstrated the independent reasonableness of following the demands of the institution.

---

[25] J Gardner, *Law as a Leap of Faith: Essays on Law in General* (Oxford, Oxford University Press, 2012) ch 1, 10.
[26] ibid 5–6.

I think that Gardner is wrong on both counts: first of all, he has not established the independence of e and i, and even if he were to demonstrate that, he would not thereby have sufficiently grounded the reasonableness of following the demands of the institution.

To claim the independence of e and i is a controversial move. After all, a more common way to think about the relation between e and i would be to think that i is somehow contained in e: by buying into friendship, I am implicitly buying into all that friendship might require, and my reason for being a friend, if, indeed, it is a good reason, indirectly gives me reasons to do everything a friend does; by deciding to be a judge, I implicitly decide to do everything a judge does, and my reason to be a judge, if, indeed, it is a good reason, gives me reason to do everything a judge does. The same applies to citizenship. For the common view, e has to be at least implicitly or inherently a reason for x. Gardner denies this common view:

> It is true that apart from his faith in God Abraham is morally wrong to kill Isaac, and with it he is morally right to kill Isaac. But his reason for having faith in God need not be, as it stands, a reason to kill Isaac.[27]

The mistake of Gardner, I think, is that here he runs together motives and reasons, or motivational and normative reasons, or the explanatory and justificatory function of reasons. Whilst there might be good (normative) reasons to have faith in a god that actually exists, there are no good (normative) reasons to have faith in a god that does not exist. And whilst there might indeed be no relation between what motivated someone to have faith in god, to join an institution or to become a friend (e_m) and the reasons provided to him by the pronouncement of that faith, institution or friendship (i_n), there is certainly a relation between the actual normative reasons one has for having faith in god, joining an institution or becoming a friend (e_n) and the normative reasons that flow from god, the institution or the friendship (i_n).

Gardner creates the false impression that the reasons for being a friend are not reasons for doing what a friend does by listing not the *actual reasons* for being a friend but only *petty motives* for being a friend. It is, of course, unsurprising that these petty motives are not even indirectly the reasons for doing what a friend does. However, the fact that there are petty motives for being a friend does not exclude the fact that there are also good reasons for being a friend. And those good reasons, whether or not they actually motivate someone to become a friend, are then indirectly reasons for doing what a friend does.

Gardner writes that one 'has a reason to make friends with someone just in case, for example, one enjoys their company'. But this is clearly wrong: if one

---

[27] ibid 6.

enjoys someone's company, one has reason to make it appear to be that person's friend. Of course, one can make oneself appear to be a person's friend by actually being that person's friend. But this is certainly not the only way to make oneself appear to be someone's friend.

So, I think that Gardner has failed to demonstrate that e and i are independent. Why is that relevant? Gardner argued that we would still need the law as the law can in principle give sound (exclusionary) reasons independently from the sound (exclusionary) reasons to have law in the first place. My argument, I think, shows that Gardner has failed to establish this independence; he has thus failed to demonstrate that the sound (exclusionary) reasons the law gives are independent from the sound (exclusionary) reasons for having law. If that is the case, however, then the reasons for having the law do all the work and the reasons that the law gives are all dependent on those reasons.

3

Law as an Order of Force or Violence

I. LAW AND VIOLENCE

THE RELATION BETWEEN law and violence[1] is mostly considered to be as follows:[2] violence is one of many social ills that need to be curtailed; one of the purposes of the law is to diminish violence and, if possible, to eradicate it; the law does this by demanding that people abstain from using force or violence; to back this demand up, the law arms itself with a threat of sanction; this threat of sanction, however, is not essential to the law being law, and the law would remain law even if it did not threaten the use of sanction; at times, the threat of sanction needs to be actualised and force needs to be employed; this employment of force, too, is not essential to the law being law.

According to this very common understanding, force or violence is an accessory to the law. We could call this understanding the moralistic attitude towards the law because it takes the law as operating in the same way as morality does. According to this attitude, the law consists mainly of demands made on us; force, conversely, only comes into play when these demands or norms fail to do their job. So first there is the law, then there is force, and even though enforcement will regularly take place, it does not need to take place for the law to be law.

---

[1] As noted in the introduction, I use the terms 'violence' and 'force' roughly interchangeably. The concept of force or violence employed in this book is a standard and literal concept of physical force and not a dialectical or figurative one. It refers to acts like killing, grasping, hitting, attacking and defending, and not to acts like saying or thinking. I also clearly distinguish the threat of force or violence from the actual use of force or violence. It is the same interpretation of force or violence as used in journals like the *Journal of Conflict Resolution*, which would define economic sanctions, for instance, as non-violent coercion. Even though I do not think much turns on a definition, force or violence could thus be quite classically defined as 'direct or indirect action applied to restrain, injure, or destroy persons or property': HL Nieburg, 'Uses of Violence' (1963) 7 *Journal of Conflict Resolution* 43, 43.

[2] See Hart and Raz, whose arguments I will discuss in some detail below. See also SJ Shapiro, *Legality* (Cambridge, MA, Harvard University Press, 2011) 169 and 175–76; H Oberdiek, 'The Role of Sanctions and Coercion in Understanding Law and Legal Systems' (1976) 21 *American Journal of Jurisprudence* 71.

Most authors subscribe to this model. There is an extreme and a moderate form of this attitude. Proponents of the extreme form claim that law and force are conceptually separated and that, accordingly, a law completely unrelated to force or violence would be conceivable as law.[3] Legal force, being a contingent feature of law, is not a suitable object for jurisprudence, but should be dealt with by sociology.

Proponents of a more moderate view would accept some kind of necessary relation between law and force, be it only an empirical or natural necessity.[4] They might concede that law without force is conceivable in a purely logical sense, but they would deny that this tells us much about the law. Just as some birds cannot fly but are nevertheless 'conceivable' as birds, so the law might be thought of independently from force or coercion. However, having left out flying or force, they would argue, we would be incapable of understanding either birds or the law. Nevertheless, even in their moderate form, these proponents would still subscribe to the main tenets of the moralistic attitude, namely that the law functions by demanding things from us and that force or violence, whilst being an important and informative accessory to the law, is still just that—an accessory. Much of the jurisprudential debate in recent decades has been between the extreme and the moderate form of the demand model.

The Pure Theory subscribes to an entirely different model. According to the Pure Theory, force is not an accessory to the law but an attribute of it: the law *is* an order of violence or force, it is a *Gewaltordnung*. Norberto Bobbio neatly brought out this point: 'In the traditional definition, force is considered a *means* for the realisation of law. According to the theory which I propose to examine, force is rather considered as the *content* of legal rules'.[5] Betti calls this an aristocratic conception of law,[6] namely, that law and right are an expression of force. For want of a better label, I will stick to it.

In what follows, I will try to elucidate and defend the aristocratic attitude.

II. THE GERM OF LAW

According to the Pure Theory, the law does not *use* force; rather, it *is* force. This can appear to be a wantonly puzzling claim. To get a clearer sense of

---

[3] I would count Raz's, Oberdiek's and parts of Hart's arguments as the extreme view. Most debates on the subject concern the relation of law and coercion, but not force. I will discuss the importance of the difference between force and coercion below.

[4] See F Schauer, *The Force of Law* (Cambridge, MA, Harvard University Press, 2015); F Schauer, 'On the Nature of the Nature of Law' (2012) 98 *Archiv für Rechts- und Sozialphilosophie* 457.

[5] N Bobbio, 'Law and Force' (1965) 49 *The Monist* 321, 321. Original emphasis.

[6] E Betti, 'La "vindicatio" romana primitiva' (1915) 39 *Il Filangieri* 321.

the nature of this claim, consider the case of theft. According to the moralistic model, what the law primarily does—how it works—is that it demands that people abstain from interfering with other people's property. Only in a second or ancillary step will this demand be backed up with a threat of sanction. In a possible third step, this threat of sanction will lead to the employment of force. Thus, according to this model, the use of force is twice removed from what the law primarily does.

The aristocratic attitude models the law's relation to force quite differently. Imagine the case where someone is about to use force to take a thing in the possession of someone else, who in turn uses force to prevent the loss of the thing. What we have here is simply a situation of two forces directed against each other. What the law according to the aristocratic model does is not to demand anything, but to assess the exercise of force. It declares the self-help of the person defending his possession against an attacker to be a lawful act:

(1) The use of force to defend one's property against an attacker is lawful.

This is all the law does in this relation. Two things need to be noted: first, the law does not directly demand anything. It does not demand that one abstain for taking someone else's property, that one use force to defend one's property, that some official come to help to defend the property or that the attacker be sanctioned or punished or otherwise coerced. Secondly, and relatedly, the force used by the defender in an important sense exists independently of the law. The defender would have likely used force to defend his property irrespective of whether rule (1) is law or not.

The law thus does not oppose the existing force or demand its eradication. Rather, it claims that a certain force is legally sanctioned and thus legal force. The main point of the law is not motivational but constitutive. It constitutes the lawfulness of a certain act. Of course, constitution, in turn, has a motivational effect. This effect, however, is a secondary one, or a side effect. What the law primarily does is declare a certain existing force lawful. This lawful force thereby becomes the force of the law. It is incorporated into the law.[7] The other force, the attack, is simply made the condition of the lawfulness of the legally sanctioned use of the force.

So the law does not have to forbid the other force or demand its cessation. This would be pointless. After all, the person defending his possession does much more than simply demand, urge or implore the attacker to cease in his attack: he uses force to stop the attacker. All the law claims is that this use of force is lawful. There is no need to demand anything. The law does not

---

[7] I will discuss how the law does that in ch 5.

need to issue commands, prohibitions or mandatory norms. As soon as the use of force against an attack is declared lawful, demanding to abstain from attacking becomes pointless or superfluous. In a similar way, Kelsen claimed that the norm 'You shall not murder' is superfluous if the norm 'He who murders ought to be punished' is valid.[8] This does not mean that the one norm excludes the other.[9] It does not mean that the norm 'You shall not murder' is *not* law. Rather, it means that positing this norm separately would be pointless since it is already, in a sense, contained in the norm stipulating the use of force. Note that the reverse is not true: if the norm 'You shall not murder' is valid, positing either 'He who murders ought to be punished' or 'Subjecting someone who has murdered to force is lawful' would not be superfluous. This relation of one-directional superfluity holds not only between the two norms, the demanding norm and the one declaring force lawful, but also between the aristocratic and moralistic attitude: the aristocratic attitude makes the moralistic attitude pointless or superfluous. It does not deny or refute what it claims, ie it does not deny that the law issues demands, it only denies that the moralistic standpoint is a comprehensive standpoint, ie that the law issues demands by issuing demands.

There is thus a sense in which the law indirectly forbids the attack of another person's property by declaring a defence by force lawful. This is not a complex philosophical issue; every halfway sensible person will understand that if the law directly allows a person to defend his possession against attack it indirectly forbids such an attack.

So the law declares the self-help of the person defending his possession against an attacker to be a lawful act. The law thus changes the meaning of the act, or it adds a new level of meaning: the act of force is no longer merely a private act of force, but is now also the enforcement of law. The law thus claims this act of force for itself, or the act of force is thus imputed to the legal community. How this change of meaning is effected will be discussed in chapter five. Note that the change of meaning occurs independently of whether the act of force has been motivated by the law or not. Furthermore, the law does not change anything about the act itself. It only changes its meaning.

---

[8] H Kelsen, *Pure Theory of Law*, trans M Knight (Berkeley, University of California Press, 1967) 55. The latter norm should have read: 'Subjecting someone who has murdered to force is lawful.'

[9] Many anglophone readers of Kelsen make this mistake. Andrei Marmor, for instance, claims that 'Kelsen's analysis misses the crucial point that the main function of most legal norms is to actually guide the conduct of the law's subjects'. However, what Marmor misses is that Kelsen is trying to explain how exactly the law does that. A Marmor, *Philosophy of Law* (Princeton, Princeton University Press, 2011) 39–40.

Without the law, what we have before us is an act of mere self-help. With the law, this act is now an act of decentralised enforcement of law.[10] According to the aristocratic model, this designation of certain pre-existing forms of violence or force as legally sanctioned is the *germ of law*.[11] It is in this germ that both the legal system and legal force co-originate. All the force the state can have emerges from this co-option of force by the law.

Law and force are thus not merely externally related, as the moralistic model suggests, but they are intimately related.

III. VIOLENCE AND SELF-HELP IN ROMAN LAW

We can get a glimpse of this 'intimate connection between *vis* and *ius*',[12] between force and law, when we have a look at Roman law. Whilst the moralistic model treats self-help as an act outside of, if not antithetical to, the law, Roman law considered self-help to be a legal institution.[13] Roman law often did not designate a specialised institution or official to take care of the enforcement of law, but rather entrusted the person directly concerned with its immediate enforcement. These enforcement acts, even if taken by private persons, were considered to be a legal institution. Talking of 'enforcement' is, of course, already misleading, as it suggests that the law is essentially separated from its enforcement—which, as I have already suggested, is not the case.

But Roman law not only gave legal licence to acts of self-help, it also suggested that more developed forms of formal legal procedure are nothing more than a ritualisation of self-help. The common legal action by which a plaintiff demanded that a defendant return a thing belonging to the plaintiff has been the so-called *vindicatio*. In this notion, not only can one still hear the Latin term

---

[10] This relation is seen by many in the case of international law: the WTO rules, for instance, are enforced not by WTO institutions, but by the members of the WTO themselves, whose coercive acts have been authorised by the WTO. The same is, of course, true for most acts of collective security under the UN system. That municipal law can be and has to be understood along the same lines, ie that there is a true continuity between national and international law, and that not only is international law fully law in the national sense, but also national law is fully law in the international sense, is usually overlooked. See OA Hathaway and SJ Shapiro, 'Outcasting: Enforcement in Domestic and International Law' (2011) Faculty Scholarship Series Paper 3850, http://digitalcommons.law.yale.edu/fss_papers/3850.

[11] For an analysis on somewhat similar lines, see R Bates, A Greif and S Singh, 'Organizing Violence' (2002) 46 *Journal of Conflict Resolution* 599.

[12] AW Lintott, *Violence in Republican Rome* (Oxford, Clarendon, 1968) 22.

[13] 'In so far as acts of self-help, particularly with regard to property, were recognized in Rome as acts in law, it seems reasonable to consider it a legal institution. Certainly it was a recognized procedure until late in the Empire': ibid 24.

for force or violence (*vi* or *vis*), but also the ritualised nature of the procedure following a *vindicatio* mirrored the force involved in the struggle over a thing:[14]

> It has long been held that the *vindicatio* that we know of inside a law court is a reproduction in its own terms of the original extrajudicial act which was the source and expression of the right now being dealt with by the law court; that in fact in such a process we can see the outlines of the extrajudicial process which was first developed to assert and express a right.[15]

V*indicatio* means *vim dicere*, to declare violence or force, 'to make a display of force'.[16] It is a claim to absolute right by superior force. Originally law was but legally sanctioned force.[17]

It does not stop here. Take the way Roman law modelled liberty rights, ie rights against the state. The moralistic attitude would have to model those rights along the following lines: first the law allocates to the citizen a liberty right against the state. This right then has to be furnished with a demand against the state not to interfere with the liberty of the citizen—say, not to arrest or kill him unlawfully. Then, in a second step, this right needs to be protected by a sanction threatened against every official who violates the right. An official who does not comply with the demand might then, in a third step, be subjected to acts of force or violence conducted by another official. Those acts of force are seen as mere accessories to the right itself. The naked right is what is the focal point to the moralistic model.

The Romans looked at it quite differently. As is well known, citizens of the Roman republic, too, had liberty rights against the state. The legal institute that protected these rights was the *presentation*, which protected Roman citizens against unlawful arrest or killing by the magistrates. How did the Romans conceive of this liberty right and where did they think it came from? Was it considered to be a naked demand made on the state, like we tend to consider human rights? Not quite. It worked via the mediation of the so-called tribunes. These were representatives of the ordinary citizens, the plebs, and were furnished with a *ius intercedendi*, a right to step in in order to protect a citizen from the legal act of a magistrate intending to arrest or kill the citizen. This *ius intercedendi* was part of the tribune's *ius auxilii*, his general right to legally aid and support the citizen against capricious acts of the magistrate. But let us

---

[14] Luzzatto presents a complex theory of evolution of vindicatio from self-help. G Luzzatto 'Von der Selbsthilfe zum römischen Prozess' (1956) 73 *Zeitschrift der Savigny-Stiftung für Rechtsgeschichte: Romanistische Abteilung* 29.

[15] Lintott (n 12) 30.

[16] M Staszków, '"Vim dicere" im altrömischen Prozeß' (1963) 80 *Zeitschrift der Savigny-Stiftung für Rechtsgeschichte: Romanistische Abteilung* 83, 107.

[17] Heusler is even more general about Nordic law: 'Denn der Gerichtsgang ist eine stilisierte Fehde' ('Legal process is a stylized feud'). A Heusler, *Das Strafrecht der Isländersagas* (Leipzig, Salzwasser, 1911) 103.

not be fooled by big Latin words. What was really important was that the tribune was legally untouchable, *sacrosanctus*, which simply meant that the tribunes were backed up by the collective force of the plebs:

> For the original oath of the plebs on the Mons Sacer must have been simply a covenant to ensure the safety of their representatives, by virtue of a promise that they would be backed by the collective force of the plebs. It was this which was the basis of the *ius auxilii*. The tribune represented the concourse of plebeians that might have otherwise assembled to help a man who used *provocatio*, shouting *Pro fidem, Quirites*, as Volero is represented as having done. If the tribune came to grief then the plebs would gather. The declaration of this sacrosanctity by law probably did not occur for some time. Again, self help rather than legal recognition was the foundation of the primitive plebeian *iuducia populi*, where a patrician who had offences against the plebs would be arraigned before an assembly which was little different in character from the council of neighbours who tried the thief.[18]

The origin of this law is plebeian; its conception, however, is aristocratic. It is summarised in a classical passage of a speech by Cicero, where he mentions 'an ancient law out of the sacred laws, which allows anyone to be put to death with impunity who has assaulted a tribune of the people'.[19]

So the Roman citizens did not have an immediate, naked right not be killed or arrested by a magistrate, just as the magistrates did not have an immediate, naked duty not to arrest or kill a citizen. Rather, the citizens had set up a system of collective self-protection against the patricians. All the law needed to do in order to set up this system of liberties is to state the following rule mentioned by Cicero:

(2)   Killing someone who has assaulted a tribune is lawful.

That something is 'lawful' simply means that it has no legal consequences. Thus, anyone who assaults a tribune can be killed with impunity, ie killing him would have no legal consequences. A tribune could thus always step in to protect a citizen without having to fear that he himself might be killed. A citizen indeed had to fear being killed or arrested by a magistrate, as the patrician magistrates had the right to hand out death penalties or fustigations without court order (*ius coercendi*).[20] A tribune, however, did not have to fear being assaulted, let alone arrested or killed, as such an assault would render the assailant outlawed or *vogelfrei*, to use a phrase taken from the Germanic legal tradition. 'If the tribune came to grief, then the plebs would gather.'[21]

[18] Lintott (n 12) 24.
[19] *Legem antiquam de legibus sacratis, quae iubeat inpune occidi eum qui tribunum pl. pulsaverit.* Cic Tull 47.
[20] G Mousourakis, *A Legal History of Rome* (London, Routledge, 2007) 12.
[21] Lintott (n 12) 24.

So Roman law did not directly demand that the liberty of Roman citizens should not be violated and then struggle to muster some force to protect it. Rather, it legally sanctioned the actually existing self-protection of the liberty of citizens. Again, the law did not need to demand any self-restraint from the magistrates. After all, the tribune did much more than simply demand, urge or implore the magistrate not to kill or arrest a citizen: the tribune used the potential force of the entire mob to actually stop the magistrate from violating the liberty of the citizen.

Viewed from the aristocratic point of view, the law is not a demand (necessarily or contingently) backed up or guaranteed by a threat of force, but is itself a balance of force. The force of the law is not a force that is in a way created by the law; it is always created by people. The law does not smash in doors; a policeman does. It is his force that the law co-opts. The law may make him smash in the door, but it can do so only by co-opting some other force: if the policeman disobeys the orders of his commander, he will ultimately be disciplined, and it is possible that in the process of this disciplinary procedures his own door will be smashed in.

The liberty rights of the Roman citizen emerged from the actual force of the mob. In the case of Roman law, the Roman citizens did not have to thank the state for any privileges generously granted to them. The actual Republican freedom is not a demand against or a gift by the state. It is loot. Roman citizens had *actual* rights based in *actual* force. As such, their law is fundamentally formalised self-help. Now, according to the Pure Theory, all law is such a balance of force.

IV. THE EFFECTIVENESS OF LAW

In contemporary jurisprudence, the fact that law is a balance of actual forces is partly expressed and partly obfuscated by the claim that for a legal system to exist it has to be 'minimally effective'. But what is meant by this effectiveness? The moralistic attitude wavers a bit on what this effectiveness requirement entails. It understands it to require that the demands issued by the legal system have to be obeyed by the people to a certain degree. However, it is unclear what obedience involves: obedience cannot mean mere compliance, as mere compliance remains uncommitted regarding the direction of fit between the law and the law-conforming behaviour: a criterion of mere compliance does not rule out that a normative system is mapped onto actual behaviour. The behaviour is then by definition compliant with the normative system, rendering it effective according to this understanding of the effectiveness requirement. According to this understanding of effectiveness, the rule 'Whatever people happen to do is according to the law' would establish an effective normative system and thus a legal system. This would certainly not represent well what we mean by effectiveness.

Effectiveness seems to touch upon a different quality than mere compliance. We would not call the above rule effective since, understood this way, effective law would not have to overcome an obstacle, it would not have to somehow put under pressure the will of people. So, it seems, effectiveness must be somehow linked to the psychological states of citizens, and we have to seek our criterion of effectiveness there. Now, the psychological state required for a legal system to be called effective cannot be found in the requirement that citizens take a critical reflective attitude towards the law or accept it. This would introduce too rigid a standard, which hardly any legal system would pass. We would end up with hardly any effective law at all, and many systems which we would want to call effective (like the system of North Korea) would be non-effective under this rendering of the requirement. Some might hesitate to qualify North Korean law as law in the full sense, but to deny it effectiveness would be quite odd.

It is thus common to try to find the psychological attitude required for a system to qualify as effective in its success of actually coercing people. Note that mere attempts to coerce or claims to coerce do not suffice here, as many clearly ineffective systems could claim or attempt to coerce. What is required for effectiveness, it seems, is systematic successful coercion.

Conceptually, however, this is a somewhat messy criterion. After all, the psychological fact of being coerced is fleeting and controversial. Since coercion depends on the motives and beliefs of the coerced, any fact can be coercive and no fact necessarily is coercive.[22]

The true problem, however, is that effectiveness is less about the psychology of the subjects than about the status of the rules. After all, a system could be effective even if it actually coerced no one. A system can be effective even if a majority of its subjects believe that they are doing what they want and are not coerced. For example, most people would claim that they abstain

---

[22] Note the vast and complex literature of coercion that tries to grapple with the fleetingness of this concept. See only R Nozick, 'Coercion' in S Morgenbesser, P Suppes and MG White (eds), *Philosophy, Science, and Method: Essays in Honor of Ernest Nagel* (New York, St Martin's Press, 1969) 440–72; A Wertheimer, *Coercion* (Princeton, Princeton University Press, 1987); H Frankfurt, *The Importance of What We Care About* (New York, Cambridge University Press, 1988) ch 7; M Gunderson, 'Threats and Coercion' (1979) 9 *Canadian Journal of Philosophy* 247; JR Pennock and JW Chapman (eds) *Nomos XIV: Coercion* (Chicago, Aldine-Atherton, 1972); G Lamond, 'Coercion, Threats, and the Puzzle of Blackmail' in AP Simester and ATH Smith (eds), *Harm and Culpability* (Oxford, Clarendon Press, 1996) 215–38; MJ Murray and DF Dudrick, 'Are Coerced Acts Free?' (1995) 32 *American Philosophical Quarterly* 118; A Ripstein, 'Authority and Coercion' (2004) 32 *Philosophy and Public Affairs* 2.

from killing or eating other humans not because they are coerced by the law but because that is what they would do even if there was no law.[23] The point of effectiveness is that even if everyone voluntarily complied and no one was actually coerced, the state would still be warranted to use force if people did not comply. The question of effectiveness is one not of motivation, but of status.

Grand Lamond is on the right track when he writes that 'it is not that coercion is necessary to account for the efficacy of law, but rather that the right to regulate coercion lies within the scope of the law's distinctive claim to authority'.[24] This, according to Lamond, also 'helps to explain the attraction of the view, developed in different ways by Bobbio and Dworkin, that law is concerned with regulating when coercion is permissible'.

It seems that the moralistic attitude has manoeuvred itself into a corner with regard to effectiveness: mere compliance cannot be the criterion of effectiveness as ineffective normative systems can be (coincidentally) complied with. Coercion cannot be the criterion of effectiveness as systems that do not actually coerce can still be effective. The acceptance of rules cannot be the criterion of effectiveness as regimes where the rules are not accepted can be effective.

The reflections on effectiveness viewed from the moralistic point of view already drive us to the edge of this view and to the cusp of the aristocratic view: effectiveness has to be understood, to use Lamond's words, as the 'right to regulate coercion', or, to use the Pure Theory's words, as 'the co-option of force by the declaration of its lawfulness'.

Let us now look at how the aristocratic model would tackle the issue of effectiveness. It is not immediately clear how rules viewed from the aristocratic point of view should be seen to be effective. If law is understood as rules about the use of force that do not directly demand anything, then how are we supposed to judge their effectiveness?

In a sense, to ask whether these rules are effective is putting the cart before the horse: these rules themselves are the bases of the effectiveness of the secondary demands based on them. As we have seen above, the rule declaring the use of force in defence of one's property lawful *is* the effectiveness of the derived secondary rule that one may defend one's property and that one must not attack someone else's property. Conversely, if one asks what makes the rule that no one ought to attack another's property an effective rule, the answer is the following: if someone attacks someone else's property, the attacked

---

[23] Schauer, *The Force of Law* (n 4) 101.
[24] G Lamond, 'Coercion and the Nature of Law' (2001) 7 *Legal Theory* 35, 56.

is legally warranted to defend his property with force. In more developed, ie centralised, legal systems, the answer would be: if someone attacked another's property, then the police would be warranted in helping the owner in his attempt to ward off the attack, or, if this does not succeed, in taking the thing back with force and in applying force against the attacker. So, in an important sense, the law *is* the effectiveness of the secondary demand based on it. Or, put differently yet again: it is not that the demand is protected by effective coercion; rather, the demands only emerge from the effectiveness of the law. The effectiveness is primary and the demand secondary.

There is also a second sense of 'effectiveness' that needs to be explored. Effectiveness is used as a criterion to distinguish 'real' rules from rules that are in a sense unreal: if a local bridge club were to demand that every human being on the planet learned to play bridge, this rule might be fully in accordance with the statutes of the club but, because of its lack of effectiveness, it would be an unreal rule. It would not help the bridge club if it threatened the use of force to guarantee this rule, because this threat would in turn be implausible. But would it help the bridge club to declare the use of force against any bridge grouch lawful? Certainly not. But have I not claimed before that in a first sense such a rule *is* or constitutes the effectiveness of the secondary rule, ie the rule to learn bridge? Now such a rule would only constitute the above-mentioned effectiveness of the secondary rule not to be a bridge grouch if it itself were somehow real, which in this case it certainly is not. What would make it real? It would only become real if it were generally applied, ie if a significant portion of people actually used it to determine which use of force is lawful and which is not. It is important to note that to say that a rule is applied does not mean that it is accepted. Even a rule which is not accepted can be applied. I can, for instance, have severe reservations against certain rules of modern English and still apply them.

Now why should a proponent of the moralistic view not make a similar argument? Could he not equally claim that the 'effectiveness' of a legal rule understood moralistically as a demand is that this demand is merely applied? Not really. A demand can be complied with, accepted or enforced and, as we have seen above, none of these yields an understanding of effectiveness. It is difficult to see how a demand could be 'applied' when this is not supposed to mean that it is complied with, accepted or actually enforced. Rules understood from the aristocratic point of view, conversely, can be applied without them being accepted, complied with or enforced: an act which had the meaning of self-help now has the meaning of 'lawful act'.

Whether general application of a rule should really be called its 'effectiveness' in a literal sense can, of course, be doubted. Effectiveness can, however, certainly be used figuratively, as it here, too, fulfils the function of allowing us to distinguish between real and unreal rules.

V. FORCE AS CONTENT OF THE LAW

Even granted all of the above, why should taking the aristocratic standpoint be preferable to taking the moralistic standpoint in general?

In what follows, I will argue that the moralistic standpoint fails as a comprehensive standpoint as it is incapable of satisfactorily distinguishing law from other non-legal normative systems.[25] What is more, between the moralistic and the aristocratic standpoint, a relation of one-directional superfluity obtains. This means that the aristocratic standpoint makes the moralistic standpoint pointless or superfluous, but not vice versa.

How can we distinguish legal systems from other normative systems, like custom, rules of morality or other non-legal institutionalised systems of rules? The claim of the Pure Theory is that if you leave force and violence out of the equation, you will not be able to come to a satisfactory way of distinguishing between law and those other normative systems. If one tries to discard force, one either fails to distinguish law from these other systems or one finds that force, as Bobbio put it, 'though thrown out of the door, seems to have re-entered through the window'.[26]

Many contemporary legal philosophers might balk at this claim referring to the forceful advocacy of Hart and Raz against anything resembling what I just claimed. In what follows, I will attack the classic arguments that the law *can* be satisfactorily distinguished from morality, custom and other non-legal institutions without any reference to force. In the last section of this chapter, I will take on the related, but different, negative claim that force *cannot* play a role in the conceptual delineation of law.

As concerns the claim that the law can be satisfactorily distinguished from morality, custom and other legal institutions, I will only briefly refer to Hart, as his stance is notoriously multifaceted, not to say, wavering: on the one hand, he was keen to stress that law should be and can be understood independently of coercion; on the other, his theory of social normativity looks very much like a theory of social coercion. And if this were not bad enough, in his later work he even came close to accepting something resembling an aristocratic model:

> I find little reason to accept … a cognitive interpretation of legal duty in terms of objective reasons or the identity of meaning of 'obligation' in legal and moral contexts which this would secure. Far better adapted to the legal case is a different,

---

[25] Ekow Yankah has made a similar argument. However, since he tries to establish the necessity of coercion and not the use of force in our concept of law, he remains firmly within the moralistic attitude. EN Yankah, 'The Force of Law: The Role of Coercion in Legal Norms' (2008) 42 *University of Richmond Law Review* 1195.

[26] Bobbio (n 5) 325–26.

non-cognitive theory of duty according to which committed statements asserting that others have a duty do not refer to actions which they have a categorical reason to do but, as the etymology of 'duty' and indeed of 'ought' suggests, such statements refer to actions which are due from or owed by the subjects having the duty, in the sense that they may be properly demanded or exacted from them. On this footing, to say that an individual has a legal obligation to act in a certain way is to say that such action may be properly demanded or exacted from him according to legal rules or principles regulating such demands.[27]

The big question here, of course, is what is meant by the difficult phrase that something 'may be properly demanded or exacted'. The notion of 'exacting something' is itself slightly mysterious. It clearly carries with it the etymological origin of *exigere*, 'to enforce, to collect', but it also has the more common meaning of 'to require, to demand'. By using the phrase 'demand and exact', Hart clearly did not want to cross the line separating him from the Pure Theory, but he nevertheless came so close that Raz referred to this passage as a 'sudden Kelsenian twist'.[28] For these reasons, Hart would turn out to be a difficult candidate to defend the claim that the realm of law can be delineated independently from force or 'exaction'. Since his arguments for why he thinks that coercion and force cannot be a useful element in the concept of law can be separated from these difficulties, I will discuss them separately in the last section of this chapter.

As concerns the claim that law can be sufficiently delineated from other non-legal normative systems without reference to force, Raz's claim is certainly the strongest and most explicit. According to Raz, what distinguishes legal systems from other institutionalised systems of norms is that legal systems are superior, comprehensive and open.[29] Now, this looks like a neat list of steadfast and decisive criteria able to tidily demarcate law from other phenomena. Unfortunately, it is not.

Let us consider the three criteria in turn. First, as Raz himself explicitly accepts, the criterion of superiority does not add anything to the list as it 'is entailed in the previous one [of comprehensiveness] and is merely an

---

[27] HLA Hart, *Essays on Bentham. Jurisprudence and Political Theory* (Oxford, Oxford University Press, 1982) 159–60.

[28] 'This sudden Kelsenian twist to Hart's view of legal duties implies that duty-imposing laws are instructions (or perhaps merely permissions) to courts to apply sanctions or remedies against people who are guilty of breach of duty. Hart himself feels uncomfortable with the conclusion he has reached ... as well he might. For if he is right then it follows either that it is not wrong to fail to fulfil one's duty or that acting wrongly is not something that one has a reason not to do': J Raz, 'Hart on Moral Rights and Legal Duties' (1984) 4 *OJLS* 123, 131. For a discussion of the Hart/Raz debate, see M Kramer, *In Defence of Legal Positivism. Law Without Trimmings* (Oxford, Oxford University Press, 1999) 81–83.

[29] J Raz, *Practical Reason and Norms* (Oxford, Oxford University Press, 1999) 149ff.

elaboration of one aspect of it'.[30] We can thus drop it from our list of criteria without loss. We are now left with only two criteria: comprehensiveness and openness.

Secondly, according to Raz, comprehensiveness is something the law possesses as soon as the law claims to possess it: a normative system is comprehensive not if it actually has authority over any type of behaviour, but if it claims authority to regulate any type of behaviour. However, what a normative system claims or does not claim to regulate is not something predetermined by its nature. If this were the case, then we would already have to know whether something is or is not in its nature a legal system in order to determine whether it actually is a legal system. This would be presupposing the answer to our question and would be arguing in a circle. So what a normative system does or does not claim is determined not by its nature, but by its pronouncements. This means that any normative system can satisfy the criterion of comprehensiveness by simply claiming authority to regulate any type of behaviour. A local bridge club could, by a valid decision of its board, claim universal jurisdiction. Of course, it would not have universal jurisdiction. However, as Raz repeatedly stresses, what matters for comprehensiveness is not the authority the system possesses, but only the authority it claims. Accordingly, since it is enough to claim comprehensiveness, our local bridge club would satisfy Raz's requirement of comprehensiveness, thus placing it only one criterion, ie the requirement of openness, away from qualifying as a legal system.

Thirdly, since any normative system can satisfy the requirement of comprehensiveness simply by claiming authority, it has to be the criterion of openness that carries all the argumentative weight of barring any one normative system, including our local bridge club from qualifying as a legal system. Can openness deliver? Unfortunately not. By openness, Raz refers to the quality of normative systems to 'contain norms the purpose of which is to give binding force within the system to norms which do not belong to it'.[31] Again, since by threat of circularity this quality cannot be either included or excluded from a normative system by dint of its very nature, whether or not a normative system exhibits the quality of openness depends on its content. Now, since our local bridge club could very well include rules that give binding force within the system of the bridge club to norms which do not belong to it, the Razian criteria cannot explain why our local bridge club cannot count as a legal system. Since this means that the rules of the local bridge could qualify as law according to Raz's list of criteria and since they certainly should not qualify as such, the list of criteria has to be flawed.

---

[30] ibid 151.
[31] ibid 152–53.

This is not a minor problem. If the criteria Raz explicitly states as the criteria of law do not allow one to correctly distinguish legal from non-legal normative systems, and since Raz is nevertheless perfectly capable of referring only to actual legal systems as legal systems (he is not biting any very hard bullets, like accepting that the bridge club actually does produce law), then it seems that he working with an unstated, implicit criterion to correctly identify the law. I think that this implicit criterion can be traced back to force.

Raz's original intuition is, of course, entirely correct. There is a sense in which legal systems are comprehensive, supreme and open. However, in trying to turn what a normative system claims to do into a criterion of the legal nature of these systems, he has, I think, made a fundamental mistake: since positive normative systems are not predetermined in what they can claim and since they can, accordingly, claim whatever they want, the claims of a normative system cannot be part of the criteria determining whether this normative system is a legal system or not. Raz's criteria seem plausible as criteria of a legal system only as he applies them to already effective normative systems. It is thus the effectiveness of the normative system that plays a crucial role in determining the legal quality of a normative system. Now, as we have seen above, effectiveness is nothing but a certain relation of force. It is thus force that has to feature in the criteria of law.[32]

So how precisely does force feature as a criterion of law? Norberto Bobbio made the very interesting suggestion that, according to Kelsen and the Scandinavian realists, what distinguishes law from other normative systems is that it consists of 'rules about force'.[33] Note that this has to be sharply distinguished from an extended imperative theory which takes the law to be rules 'guaranteed by force'. Actually, Bobbio comes very close to what I called the aristocratic attitude. He starts his argument with the following considerations:

> The content of the rules of chess is the game of chess, just as the content of grammar is speaking; of rhetoric, persuasion; of aesthetics, poetry; of logic, thought; of fashion, dressing. But is there a type of behaviour which, different from any other type of behaviour, is the proper content of legal rules? Is there a legal behaviour of which law is the rule, in the same way that there is a linguistic behaviour of which grammar can be said to be the rule?[34]

---

[32] I will discuss Raz's arguments why force not only does not but cannot play a role in our definition of law below.

[33] Bobbio (n 5) 322.

[34] ibid 327.

'Social life' cannot be the specific legal content, as social life 'is not the content of legal rules, but only the context in which they operate'.[35] The solution that Bobbio credits to the Pure Theory is, of course, force:

> If law is the body of rules which regulate the exercise of force, this means that force is the specific object of legal rules, in the same way as language is the specific object of grammar.[36]

> In the traditional definition, force is considered a means for the realization of law. According to the theory which I propose to examine, force is rather considered as the content of legal rules.[37]

This is by and large correct, but an important point needs to be clarified: it is not sufficient to stipulate that legal rules have a specific content. As we have seen, a positive rule can have any content. The rules of a local bridge club could make the use of force their content and declare a certain use of force lawful, just as they could declare the use of certain words ungrammatical. These declarations, whilst in line with the statutes of the bridge club, would not be real because they would not be 'effective' in the above-given sense, ie the sense that the rules of a local bridge club would not be generally applied to acts of force or the general use of language.

The law thus regulates force and violence in a similar way to how grammar regulates language: it tells us which expressions of force or, in the case of grammar, speech and writing are lawful; the 'effectiveness' (in inverted commas) of these rules can be found in them actually being applied; the motive for applying the rules is completely irrelevant for them actually being applied; thus, in order to be applied, these rules do not need to be accepted, ie they can be applied even if everyone thought that different rules should be applied; equally, since coercion depends on psychological motives, coercion does not play a role. In contrast to the rules of grammar, the 'effectiveness' of legal rules, ie the fact that they are actually applied, is the basis for the effectiveness (without inverted commas) of the secondary demands based on these rules: the fact that everyone applies the legal rule to the effect that force can be legally used against an attack of one's property *is* the effectiveness of the secondary rule that no one ought to attack someone else's property. So, whilst the moralistic model starts with the demand and then struggles for effective enforcement of this demand, the aristocratic model starts with effectiveness (allowing the use of force) and from that it derives the demand, which is secondary.

What thus matters is not only that legal rules have force as their content, which is certainly true, but that they have force as their content in the same

---

[35] ibid 327.
[36] ibid 328.
[37] ibid 321.

sense that the actual rules of grammar have language as their content. What is thus required is that the rules for them to be legal rules have to be effective, ie generally applied.

VI. LAW AND STATE

Finding the germ of law in a certain interpretation of force or violence, and thus discovering legal rule and legal force to be co-original, tells us something important about the relation of law and state: it corroborates the thesis of the Pure Theory about the identity of law and state.[38]

Part and parcel of the moralistic view of the law is the conviction that the law as a system of demands made on us needs to be clearly distinguished from the state as the force that aims to guarantee the enforcement of these demands. The state is understood as the sociological force behind the law, and the state creates, administers and enforces the law. According to this view, the law could very well exist without the state and the state could exist without law.

The aristocratic attitude challenges this view. According to it, the state is but the force declared lawful by the law. What distinguishes primitive societies of self-help from modern bureaucracies is not the kind of legal regulation, but only the degree of centralisation. Let us look at the rules regulating murder first. In a primitive legal system, the only rule regulating murder might be the following.

(3) Killing someone who has killed someone else unlawfully is lawful.

Note that in this context 'unlawful' is not a substantive but an entirely negative or dependent term, ie its content is parasitic on the term 'lawful'. This means the following: according to rule (3), it would be unlawful to kill someone who either (i) has not killed anyone at all or who (ii) has not killed someone unlawfully. Taken in isolation, option (ii) leads to a vicious logical circle, since in order to find out what 'unlawful' means we would already have to know what it means. This circle in option (ii), however, does not pose a problem as the meaning of 'unlawful' is sufficiently anchored in option (i). The result is the following: if no one had killed anyone, then the question of the lawfulness of killing does not arise. The first killing, however, is certainly unlawful according to our dependent definition, because as a first killing it cannot be of anyone who has himself killed someone, thus fulfilling above criterion (i). Killing the

---

[38] For an extended defence of the identity thesis see L Vinx, *Hans Kelsen's Pure Theory of Law* (Oxford, Oxford University Press, 2007).

first killer would then be lawful. Now if someone killed the killer of the first killer, option (ii) would come into play, rendering this third killing unlawful: the second killer has killed someone (thus ruling out option (i)), but he has not done so unlawfully.

In an ongoing series of revenge killings, the simple rule (3) allows us to distinguish lawful killings from unlawful ones, thus allowing us to distinguish the killings that can be imputed to the law, which is the law's killing, from the killing which occurs in violation of the law. By marking out any killing as either lawful or unlawful, as either enforcing the law or violating it, this rule actually covers all killing. It is in this sense that even a primitive rule like rule (3) monopolises the use of force—at least in respect to killing. What we need to separate from this monopolisation of the use of force through the law is the centralisation of the use of force. A primitive self-help system installed by rule (3) certainly lacks centralisation.

Let us get a clearer understanding of this important difference and relation between monopolisation and centralisation of the use of violence: the monopolisation of the use of violence is regularly picked out by sociologists in the wake of Weber as the defining feature of the state.[39] However, what is monopolisation supposed to mean? Clearly, monopolisation cannot mean that no force at all is used any more. After all, if no force is used at all, there would be nothing to be monopolised. Equally, however, monopolisation cannot mean that only the state actually uses force: for why would the state need to use force if no one resisted the state by force? This makes the concept of monopolisation itself more difficult than it has seemed. If monopolisation cannot mean that no force is used at all or that only the state actually uses force, what is left? Monopolisation can only mean the following: only the state is *allowed* to use force, the state has a monopoly on lawful or allowed force.[40] This, however, not only means that it is only the state that is allowed to use force, but also, more importantly, that whoever is allowed to use force belongs to the state. Because of this relation, it is the case that as soon as we have law we have a (rudimentary) state and the monopolisation of force is already completed. Since the use of force is monopolised by definition as soon as we have law, monopolisation does not work for the intended purpose of distinguishing, in Weber's terminology, states from non-states, or, in a better terminology, civil states from savage states. This job of distinguishing is actually done only by the notion of centralisation: whilst both in a civil and in a savage state the use

---

[39] See M Weber, *Weber's Rationalism and Modern Society. New Translations on Politics, Bureaucracy, and Social Stratification*, trans T Waters (New York, Palgrave, 2015) ch 7, 136.

[40] Raz also misses the point of monopolisation. See J Raz, *Between Authority and Interpretation. On the Theory of Law and Practical Reason* (Oxford, Oxford University Press, 2009) 172.

of force is monopolised, it is only in the former that the use of force is also centralised, ie administered by a central organ.[41]

Take the case that we have an ongoing series of revenge killings between feuding tribes. Rule (3) allows us to interpret this series as a series of successive breaches of law and law enforcements, as a series of crimes and punishment. Rule (3) thus allows us to identify within the series of successive killings lawful 'police acts' and unlawful 'crimes'. The law thus monopolises but does not yet centralise the use of force.

We tend to think that the law monopolises force by forbidding its use and then somehow preventing its use. This presupposes that the law already has force. However, the law, strictly speaking, does not have any actual power, so cannot force anyone to do anything. The law is language.

Rather than forbidding and preventing the use of force, the law monopolises force by declaring a certain force legally irrelevant. It thus decides which social force is its own force. Thus, the law does not monopolise force by somehow mustering an irresistible actual power and commanding everyone to refrain from using force; rather, it declares a certain social force to be the legal force.

The law identifies the sovereign force among the existing forces. The law does not create a consolidated force; rather, it consolidates force by declaring the prevalent historic force to be its own force. In so far as the law never needs to exert itself, it does not have to dominate social power or fight an opposition. All it needs to do is interpret an already existing social force as being the legal force.

The case of ongoing revenge killings between feuding tribes, viewed sociologically, is certainly a state of war. Viewed legally, however, it is a succession of crimes and punishment, and thus peace-keeping. Peace-keeping presupposes peace. So the rules allow us to interpret the situation of war as peace. Morality demands that there be peace. The law makes peace by declaring it. The law does not make peace by somehow abolishing the use of force but by declaring a certain force to be its own force. It makes peace by monopolising force. This peace is certainly only a peace in name, it is a messy peace. It does, however, need to be first called a peace in order to then be 'tidied up' by the process of centralisation.

But are not our contemporary systems of centralised enforcement substantively different? Well, the difference between a system of self-help and a system of state enforcement is not one of kind but only of degree, namely the degree of centralisation.

If we want to centralise the application of a decentralised rule applied by everyone on everyone, all we have to do is to add a condition to our rule. The condition which the original rule (3) set down for the lawfulness of killing someone was that the person killed had himself unlawfully killed

---

[41] See also Vinx (n 38) 42–43.

someone else. A centralised version of this rule would have to somehow add the condition that a certain organ determines that the person in question has killed someone else. In order to get a centralised rule, we would have to somehow replace the conditions 'if someone kills someone unlawfully' with 'if a competent organ declares that someone has killed someone unlawfully'. I will explain how exactly this is done below.

What needs to be noted here is the relation of the two conditions. Simply adding the declaration of a fact to the fact itself would not result in centralisation, but in a two-pronged system of centralisation and decentralisation—if a rule had as its condition for the lawfulness of the use of force that 'someone has actually killed someone and that a competent organ declares that someone has actually killed someone'—this would allow for a situation in which the competent organ declares that A has killed B, yet C knows (or believes he knows) that in fact A has not killed B. Centralisation is thus first and foremost a remedy to perspectivism and the problem of opinion. In order for the determination of the competent organ to have this effect, it has to be understood as being constitutive and not merely declaratory. Understanding the utterance of a competent organ in a merely declaratory sense would mean that we do not take the organ as determining what is the case but we take the facts themselves as continuing to determine what is the case and we take the organ only as declaring what is determined in the facts themselves. This, however, means nothing other than that we ultimately want everyone to determine by himself what is the case. To claim that 'the facts themselves' decide the case only means that everyone can decide the case for himself. Someone has to decide. The choice the law has to make is not between letting the facts themselves decide and letting an organ decide; it is between letting everyone decide and letting someone decide. The difference between declaratory and constitutive statements is thus based on the difference between decentralised and centralised determination of facts.

So how exactly does the law replace one condition with another? In order to establish a system of centralised state enforcement, one does not need to rescind rule (3) but only add another rule that relates to vigilante justice. This added rule, too, is not formulated as a naked demand on people to abstain from taking justice into their own hands. Rather, it follows the same aristocratic logic of declaring the use of force lawful where certain conditions are fulfilled. This time, the condition for the lawfulness of the use of force is that someone has killed someone else (who himself might have killed someone) without being authorised by a judge to make this killing:

(4)   Killing someone (φ) who has killed someone else lawfully (ρ) is itself lawful if the historically first killing (ρ) has occurred without being authorised by a judge.

The recursive nature of this rule has the effect that now *any* killing has to be authorised by a judge in order *not* to have the effect of rendering a killing of the last killer lawful: imagine that A killed B, who had not killed anyone. Now, if C kills A, this would be lawful according to rule (3). However, the lawfulness of this killing would have the effect that killing C would be unlawful. Now rule (4) does not take back this rule, it only further qualifies its effect: if D killed C, this killing would be lawful if C had not been authorised by a judge to kill A. Whether C is a family member of B who wants revenge or whether he is a public executioner who is unrelated to B and just does his job does not matter for the applicability of rule (4). What matters is that if there is no authorisation, then D killing C would be lawful. However, rule (4) also applies to D's killing of C! So D would need to be authorised by a judge to avoid his killing of C having the result of rendering a killing of himself lawful, say, by E. But again, rule (4) also applies to E, and so on.

Note that rule (4) does not limit the lawfulness of killing; rather, it expands it. Under Rule (3) alone, killing C would not be lawful. Under rule (4), though, killing C would be lawful! This demonstrates the seemingly paradoxical result that the law, understood aristocratically, can restrict the use of force or violence by allowing it. Of course, it is not really paradox, as the law is not a demand guaranteed by force but a balance of force, ie the law uses existing force against force, it pushes back force not with language but with force.

The authorisation by the judge can stipulate who is to be killed, by whom and in what way. Any killing of someone outside the authorisation renders the killer himself liable to being killed even in the case where his killing would otherwise be lawful, ie where he kills someone who has unlawfully killed someone else.

We can also have a look at the less savage example of the centralisation of the protection of property, where the rule

(5) Using force against someone who unlawfully uses force to take one's property is lawful.

is accompanied by the following rule in a similar manner to rule (3) being accompanied by rule (4):

(6) Using force against someone who lawfully uses force against someone else is lawful if the lawful use of force has occurred without being authorised by a judge.

This is how, according to the aristocratic model, the centralisation of the use of force is effected. Note that in each case the force is still the same and that the law still operates according to the same logic: under certain conditions, the use of force is lawful. Even in the more complex rendering it is still the case that it is not the law that creates the force, but the force always has to be created by someone, be it a family member who takes revenge, a police officer who does his job or a henchman who satisfies his perverse bloodlust. The complexity of the legal system does not change the basic structure of the functioning of the law. The whole complexity of the legal system enters only through the door of the specific conditions which are added to condition the lawfulness of the use of force: these conditions might not only stipulate that the use of force has to be authorised by a judge, but also make explicit by reference to legislation who counts as a judge and which instances of use of force the judge can author- ise, and might further make explicit by means of constitution-formation how these requirements can be changed. The entire hierarchy of norms, ranging from the law authorising the use of force, via court organisation rules and criminal law to the constitution, is brought in through the door of these condi- tions of the lawfulness of the use of force.

So, in a centralised rule, a judge gets to decide what the facts of the case are, and the result of coercion being lawful depends not on the facts themselves, but on the decision of the judge. What we have in the decentralised and cen- tralised versions of the rule are two conditionals, two statements which make the occurrence of two different facts the conditions of the lawfulness of the use of force. Now, even in the centralised version of the law, the application of the conditional (ie the establishment of the fact that conditions the inter- pretation of killing someone as lawful) is still entrusted to everyone. It cannot be otherwise. Thus, even the centralised version of the rule is applied in a decentralised manner. Whereas in the original, decentralised version everyone was called to establish for himself that someone has actually killed someone else, the centralised version entrusts to everyone the decision of whether the competent organ has actually declared that someone has taken the life of someone else. Now, it is often much easier to reach agreement on the fact that someone has declared something rather than on the fact that someone has unlawfully killed someone. The controversy of the decentralised determina- tion 'What has really happened back then?' is reduced to the less onerous, yet still decentralised, determination of 'What has the judge said and is he really a judge?'

This centralisation by decentralised indicates that an understanding of the law which focuses on commands or demands is incomplete. The com- mand enters the legal stage as the content of the decree of the judge (or the legislator). However, as we have seen, the command of the judge is but a con- dition of the applicability of a rule which has to be applied by everyone, ie has to be applied in a decentralised manner. The command thus always rests on a more fundamental rule, albeit one that cannot be understood as a command or a demand.

We can thus see how the legal system is built from the bottom up. Even though abstract qualities of the law, like validity or legality, might be explained and understood as flowing down from the basic norm, the law's normative relevance is only seen and confirmed as soon as it reaches the 'ground', the use of force. This ground-floor operation can be seen and remains the same whether we face a primitive one-storey system or a complex multi-layered high-riser. Equally in every case, irrespective of the complexity of the system, we will find a basic norm, which just states the obvious: it states that law is law, namely that 'the use of force is to be applied according to the law'.[42] The basic norm thus simply restates the concept of law we have developed here. In this sense, the basic norm is but the placeholder of legal philosophy as a norm, it is the concept of law as a legal norm. This norm only takes on the guise of mystery as long as it sits detached on top of a complex, layered hierarchy and is thus removed from the basic operation of the law. If we take a one-storey system consisting only of rules like rule (3), stipulating that the use of force against a killer is lawful, then a presupposed basic norm stipulating that the lawfulness of the use of force is to be determined in accordance with the law appears quite straightforward.

All the other classic doctrines of the Pure Theory, the hierarchy of the legal system, the dynamic nature of the creation of law, the doctrines of authorisation, of alternative authorisation, etc, emerge from this injection of legal complexity via the conditions for the lawfulness of the use of force.

However, the introduction of all legal acts, from the framing of the constitution to legislation to adjudication as mere conditions of the lawfulness of the use of force poses a classic problem: how are these conditions to be distinguished from the behaviour which also conditions the lawfulness of the use of force but which I argued is, if only in a secondary sense, forbidden by the law? If all legal acts, including legislation and adjudication, are mere conditions of the lawfulness of the use of force, why are they not equally, if only in a secondary sense, deemed to be forbidden?

Official acts are not deemed to be forbidden since the secondary sense of being forbidden does not attach to something merely being a condition to the use of force but derives only from a prudential calculation of someone faced with the rule, someone who wants to know what to do in the face of the law. We could call this person, in line with Hart's analysis the *puzzled man*: if I am pondering whether or not to kill B and take into account that, according to rule (3), my killing of B would render anybody else's killing of me lawful, then I would already know that in a legal sense I ought not to kill B. The explicit legal rule, 'No one ought to kill anybody', would not be invalid or inexistent,

---

[42] Kelsen rendered the basic norm simply as force is to be applied 'under certain conditions and in a certain way': H Kelsen, *Introduction to the Problems of Legal Theory. A Translation of the First Edition of the Reine Rechtslehre or Pure Theory of Law*, trans BL Paulson and S Plaulson (Oxford, Clarendon Press, 2002) 57.

it would be superfluous; it would be pointless to explicitly posit this rule. The same cannot be said in relation to the judge: if a judge faces the situation of whether or not to authorise the killing of me after I have killed someone without awaiting his authorisation, he does not, even as a *puzzled judge*, come to the conclusion that in general he ought not to authorise the use of force. What he ought or ought not to do legally in a secondary sense is determined not by a rule like rule (4), but by a rule attaching to his abuse of power sanctions and ultimately the use of force against him.

How is all of this related to the identity of law and the state? In the Pure Theory, we can find two approaches to arguing in favour of the identity of law and state. One argues from the top down, the other argues from the bottom up. The classic top-down approach first asks what the state is:[43] certainly the state cannot exist beyond what it does. Stipulating an unobservable entity beyond state acts would belong more to a mystical or metaphysic inquiry than to a sober scientific one. So the state has to be identified with what it does—it substantially consists of acts of state. The question then is: what qualifies an act as an act of state? There are three candidates for answering this question: it could be (i) informal rules, (ii) sociological rules or (iii) legal rules that determine which acts of which persons are imputed to the state. However, on closer inquiry, it turns out that both the informal and the sociological rules are mere heuristics tracing the legal rules. This comes to light as soon as one considers the case of a possible conflict between these different sets of rules. If there is conflict between these rules, if they were to come to different conclusions about which acts count as acts of state, then the legal rules would prevail. 'According to the identity thesis, an act performed by some human being will qualify as an act of state only if it conforms to the legal norms that purport to govern the relevant category of acts of state.'[44] It is thus the law that conclusively determines which acts count as acts of state, and it is also the law that determines the meaning and thus the content of these acts. It is in this sense that Kelsen claims that the law *is* the state.

The argument presented in this book reaches the same conclusion but via the opposite route. It starts at the very bottom of the law, ie at the point where the law relates to something which is not, in turn, the creation of new law. This is where the law relates directly to the use of actual force. The argument for the identity of the law and the state viewed from this side of the legal hierarchy looks like this: even if we were to understand the state as the force 'behind' the law, an inquiry into how the law actually regulates the use of force shows us that this force has the same origin as the law itself. Both emerge from

---

[43] It is best explained by Vinx (n 38).
[44] ibid 19.

the germ of law, which is the interpretation of the use of force or violence as lawful. This interpretation allows us to take certain forms of use of force as lawful and thus attributable to the state. This 'state' might at first be a decentralised state, which is then consolidated by the function of centralisation, described above. What justifies calling both a state is that the difference between the centralised and the decentralised state is one of degree, not of kind.

The 'state' is the group of people who are involved in the concretisation of the conditions of the lawfulness of the use of force and who are engaging in the lawful use of force.

VII. CRITICISM

Readers brought up in the classic Oxford school of jurisprudence must have been shifting in their seats while reading what I have just claimed, as all of this must seem straightforwardly wrong. Have not Hart and Raz once and for all laid to rest the idea that law is necessarily connected to sanctions? Is not the claim that the law is an order of force or violence demonstrably false?

In order to deal with this criticism, I have to first make sure that I have stated the claim of the Pure Theory clearly: it does not argue that the law is necessarily related to sanctions or coercion, but only that the law is necessarily related to the use of force.[45] I concur with the Hartian result that it is pointless to argue that coercion is a necessary part of the law. But I think that this has less to do with the law and more to do with coercion: since coercion understood as 'bending someone's will'[46] is at least partially a psychological fact dependent on both the desires and motives of the person supposedly coerced, we can never know a priori if an act or a fact is coercive. To be coerced, the person coerced needs to co-operate in the coercive process to a certain degree. No one can coerce someone else entirely unilaterally. Thus, no description of an act can count as coercive by itself.

---

[45] Some authors argue that the use of force should also be considered to count as coercion. Whether or not this is true, however, is not relevant for my argument. The issue is not whether we call the use of force coercion but whether force is a necessary part of the law. G Lamond, 'Coercion, Threats and the Puzzle of Blackmail' in AP Simester and ATH Smith (eds), *Harm and Culpability* (Oxford, Clarendon Press, 1996) 215–38; G Lamond, 'The Coerciveness of Law' (2000) 20 *OJLS* 39; MD Bayles, 'A Concept of Coercion' in JR Pennock and JW Chapman (eds), *Nomos XIV: Coercion* (Chicago, Aldine-Atherton, 1972) 16–29; M Gunderson, 'Threats and Coercion' (1979) 9 *Canadian Journal of Philosophy* 247.

[46] See, eg, A Sangiovanni, 'The Irrelevance of Coercion, Imposition, and Framing to Distributive Justice' (2012) 40 *Philosophy and Public Affairs* 79, 81; R Nozick, 'Coercion' in Morgenbesser et al (n 22) 440–72.

As Hart himself points out, 'the person threatened is literally able to choose whether to act as instructed or suffer the threatened harm, so that a choice exists'.[47] In a literal sense, therefore, we can only coerce free agents. I would not say that I am coercing my car or computer to do anything. So coercion not only allows for a certain degree of voluntariness, it presupposes it. But if this is the case, then, irrespective of all other factors of coercion, whether or not some action counts as coercion or not depends not only on the act itself and the intention of the coercer, but also on the will (and the motives and beliefs) of the coerced. Thus, an attempted coercion could be unsuccessful and an unsuccessful attempted coercion could fail to count as coercion at all. For example, a person pointing a gun at me and saying 'Your money or your life' is usually considered to be coercing me. If I were especially brave and strong willed, and were to resist him in order to not bow down to coercion, then the coercive act might have failed; but whatever the result, if I still 'felt the pressure', it would not be absurd to still speak of coercion, even if unsuccessful. However, if the person were trying to coerce me with something I secretly wished for, then the unsuccessful coercion would not even count as coercion. If the gunman approached me on my way to a bridge from which I was planning to jump, or in a situation where I were so tired of life or in so much pain that in shooting me he would actually be doing me a favour, then there would be no sense in which he would be coercing me at all. This means that *any* attempted coercion can not only fail to actually lead to the coerced behaviour, but it can also fail to count as coercion at all.

In other words, one and the same system of norms can be either coercive or non-coercive, depending on the people it applies to and their motives. If coercion were indeed a necessary element of the concept of law, then in one case we would have to call this normative system law whilst in the other we would have to withhold that label. This would be very odd.

One could try to avoid this difficulty by making reference to *attempted* coercion instead of *actual* coercion. However, this would solve the psychological puzzle on the side of the coerced only by introducing the same puzzle on the side of the coercer. Alternatively, one could try to make reference to the fact that the law typically coerces, as propounded by Frederick Schauer.[48] However, whilst certainly telling us something about the law, such an empirical generalisation cannot solve the conceptual dilemma.

There is indeed a link between coercion and the use of force. This link is fully contingent: one can certainly use the threat of brute force to coerce people,

---

[47] HLA Hart and AM Honoré, *Causation in the Law*, 2nd edn (Oxford, Oxford University Press, 1985) 157.

[48] Schauer, *The Force of Law* (n 4).

and some argue that the use of brute force constitutes coercion; however, one can do things with brute force other than coerce, and one can coerce people with other things than the threat or exercise of brute force. One can coerce people with sublime psychological force, with the withdrawal of affection or the like. Conversely, one can use force simply to annoy people with no intention of coercing them.

So the Hartian case against coercion being a conceptual or necessary element of the law is granted by the Pure Theory of Law. What the Pure Theory does not grant is that the same is true for the use of force.

Without the reference to force, the Pure Theory claims, legal systems cannot be distinguished from other normative, but non-legal, systems. That this is the case is illustrated by Hart's own line of argument, which, after stressing that law without coercion is conceivable, ends up accepting that coercion is part of the concept of law: what distinguishes law from etiquette is the seriousness of social pressure. This, however, cannot distinguish law from moral or religious standards. Here Hart accepts that what distinguishes law from morality is that in the former case 'physical sanctions are prominent or usual among the forms of pressure'.[49] Since this prominence or frequency of physical sanctions is the only element that allows us to distinguish law from other 'serious' normative systems, it has to be part of the concept of law. Coercion was thrown out via the door, but is let back in via the window. Hart even comes close to seeing law in terms of the content of law and accepting that legal rules are basically rules about force or violence: 'Characteristically, rules so obviously essential as those which restrict the free use of violence are thought of in terms of obligation'[50] and thus in terms of law. But, of course, for Hart this is not the only or central content of law.

The dialectics of Hart's demand of '*voluntary* cooperation in a *coercive* system'[51] shows us the entire logic of that relation condensed into a single phrase. Hart here restates his classic position: first there is the demand, directed at voluntary co-operation. If that does not work, then coercion steps in. This coercive background is necessary, it is often argued, mainly for the reason of assurance: I can only co-operate voluntarily whilst still acting rationally if I am assured that others are made to co-operate if they do not co-operate voluntarily. This, it is argued, does not make coercion or force a necessary element of the law. However, *assurance* is not only an other-regarding concept, but a reciprocal one. That means it not only operates against others, but also assures others that I will be forced to co-operate if I fail to co-operate voluntarily.

---

[49] HLA Hart, *The Concept of Law*, 2nd edn (Oxford, Oxford University Press, 1994) 86.
[50] ibid, 87.
[51] ibid, 198. Original emphasis.

It is not the case that the law directs its benevolent, merely standard-setting side at me and its fierce, assuring, force-justifying side at others. It directs both at both. Everyone is assured against everyone. The idea of 'assurance' tries to suggest that the use of force is but a second option, a plan B: first we try to create co-operation by urging and demanding, then, if that does not work, we move to assuring. But this cannot be maintained. The point of the Pure Theory is the following: as soon as we have assurance, then demanding and urging are superfluous. If a demand is assured, then assurance renders the demand superfluous or pointless because the law demands *by means of* assurance.

So, even if one wanted to understand the law as simply setting standards, in order for these standards to be legal standards, they need to be enforced or at least assured. Accordingly, the law as law not only sets standards of behaviour, it sets those standards in a certain law-like manner: it sets them by declaring the use of force lawful. However, as soon as we have seen how the law sets standards, ie by declaring the use of force lawful, the standard-setting function is less interesting, because it has become pointless when taken in isolation.

But let us not be content with dealing with Hart's own arguments. The gist of his theory has been further developed by Raz and extended to the use of force. I will now turn to his rendering of the topic.

Raz asks if 'it is possible for there to be a legal system in force which does not provide for sanctions or which does not authorise the enforcement by force'. His famous answer is that it is 'humanly impossible but logically possible'.[52]

I will argue that it is both logically impossible and theoretically pointless. Again, it needs to be stressed that I grant Raz the claim that a legal system that does not provide for sanctions might indeed by logically possible: as discussed above, the use of sanction as coercion cannot be conceptually linked to the law. The situation is different when it comes to use of force. Raz muddies the water by using the slightly odd phrase 'enforcement by force': whether the use of force counts as the 'enforcement' of certain legal demands is, as we have seen, a secondary question to be answered only from the point of view of the legal subject in relation to which the use of force is declared lawful. What the law does is not to enforce by force, but simply to declare the use of force lawful. And irrespective of what counts as enforcement, the law cannot possibly be understood as law without this declaration of lawful of the use of force.

How does Raz go about arguing that a legal system that does not authorise force is 'logically possible'? He does so along the lines of Hart by arguing that such a legal system is conceivable:

And yet we can imagine other rational beings who may be subject to law, who have, and who could acknowledge that they have, more than enough reasons to obey the

---

[52]   Raz (n 29) 158. For a similar but weaker claim see Raz (n 40) 158.

law regardless of sanctions. Perhaps even human beings may be transformed to become such creatures. It is reasonable that in such a society the legislator would not bother to enact sanctions since they would be unnecessary and superfluous. If such a normative system has all the features of a legal system described above then it would be recognised as one despite its lack of sanctions.[53]

I think this is all wrong, for a number of reasons, some of them minor, some of them fatal.

First, in this section, Raz suddenly shifts his focus entirely to sanctions and leaves out reference to the authorisation of force. Whether this is because he saw that his argument could not be sustained in relation to the use of force remains speculation.

Secondly, Raz focuses on the empirical question of motivation. Angels and the future humans (are they communards living in a communist Utopia where the state has withered away?) may indeed not need to be motivated by sanctions or the threat of force, but this is not the relevant question. The relevant question is whether use of force would ever be lawful against those future humans. There are only two possibilities, both of which run counter Raz's argument. (i) If some use of force, ie some rudimentary form of self-defence against direct attack, were still lawful in our Utopian society, then we would, again, have a system of force. What Raz calls 'the law' in this Utopian society, ie the co-ordination and decision-making procedures and institutions, would certainly be tied up with this system of force. Note that it does not matter whether people would actually have occasion to resort to self-defence. The question is not whether the use of force is likely, but only whether it is lawful. (ii) If, on the other hand, Raz were to retreat to the extreme position that in his Utopian society no use of force at all was deemed lawful, then all the paradoxes of a fully pacifist society would emerge: if no use of force were deemed lawful, then all use of force would be unlawful. However, this unlawfulness would not have any meaning, since it would certainly not allow the use of force against unlawful force. So, whilst any use of force were unlawful, any attempt to curtail the use of force would be unlawful, too. One might argue that this would not matter in the Utopian society, as no one would attack anyone so no one would need to defend themselves against attack. However, one might want to defend oneself not only against a malicious attack, but also against an innocent or accidental attack. Raz would certainly not want to push the Utopian quality of his society so far as to claim that innocent, accidental attacks would be excluded in principle. One could only guarantee the impossibility of innocent or accidental attacks by making any interaction between people impossible. To remain coherent, the Utopian

---

[53] Raz (n 29) 159.

law would have to declare the use of force even against accidental force unlawful. But would that make any sense? Imagine that the marble sculpture that my neighbour built got loose and was rolling down the hill, thereby threatening my entire family. Would I have to let it just roll on? Or would I be allowed to use force against the other person's (not property, but) product?

Thus, even in the Utopian case, some use of force will be lawful. Anything else would be absurd. On top of that, one can very well imagine a law where the actual use of force never manifests itself but remains entirely latent. This, however, would be an accidental quality of this legal system, ie one entirely dependent on how the subjects chose to behave. Whether the actual use of force is latent or manifest does not change the legal rule stipulating that if certain conditions are fulfilled the use of force is lawful. It does not matter to the law whether these conditions are actually fulfilled or not, and even if they are fulfilled it does not matter to the law whether legal force is actually used. Just because the use of force is permitted does not mean that it actually occurs.

So, as we have seen, the question of law's relation to force is not an empirical or psychological one relating to motivation, but is entirely a question of status. The question is not whether angels or subjects living in a communist Utopia would need to be motivated by force. Rather, the legal question is only one of the legal status of the use of force. The legal question would be this: would the use of force be lawful if the angel or communist acted against his nature and against the law? The likeliness of this action, or the fact that this would be unlikely, does not change the status: if the angel or communist acted in violation of the law, the use of force would be lawful. This is a normative question, not a factual one.

To illustrate this point, let us take the case of a highly religious community within the state. These people happen to never break the criminal law. Does this mean that, for that community, if they broke the law the use of force would not be allowed? Certainly not. Now what if all but one small minority of crooks in a state always followed the criminal law? Would this mean that the law does not allow the use of force against law breakers? Certainly not. What if, instead of a small minority, there were only one person that ever broke the law? What if, finally, for a long time no one broke the law—would the use of force no longer be allowed if it is broken? Raz would have to show that the use of force is not lawful in certain circumstances in order to demonstrate that force is not a necessary element of the law, that law without force is conceivable. He has not done that, because, of course, he cannot do it.

Force is part of the law not because of some arbitrary feature of the human psyche or man's motivational set-up. It is not a lamentable consequence of crookedness of human nature. It is not an anthropological consequence, but a logical one. It is part of the law because of a logical asymmetry between wickedness and goodness, or, to be more precise, between law breaking and law abiding. The mere possibility of law breaking has normative consequences, whereas the mere possibility of law abiding does not. I call this the *Hobbesian crux*. The law argues that under certain conditions the use of force is lawful. This means that it attaches the use of force to the mere possibility of certain conditions. The mere possibility of breaking the law makes force necessary. So the sheer fact that the law is actually not broken does not exclude force. Raz would have to show that breaking the law is impossible in that situation. But if it is impossible, then either there is no law or there is force in play.

It is surprising that Raz does not see this. Law necessarily licenses the use of force. Now, whether or not force is ever actually used is an entirely empirical question. In societies of angels, force might never be used, but this does not change the fact that the law would license force if certain conditions were fulfilled.

Thirdly, Raz argues that in angelic or communist societies the 'legislator would not bother to enact sanctions'. If the legislator bothering or not bothering determines whether something is part of the concept of law, then by the same logic straightforward mandatory norms like 'No one ought to kill anyone' would not be part of the concept of law, since it is the actual legislator, and not a fictitious one existing merely in Raz's imagination, that does not bother to enact such rules. Early Germanic law, for instance, could do without prescriptions.

> The rules of early Germanic law from the very beginning were conditional judgements (*Si quis ...*). To conceive of the Germanic law as a sum of orders or prescriptions would be a violent modern fiction. Legal commands and prescriptions are essentially foreign to the Germans.[54]

Similarly, in modern law, the legislator does not bother to set down mandatory norms, as it is enough to set down sanctions for certain behaviour. Does this mean that legal systems without mandatory norms are 'logically and humanly possible'? Not really.

Fourthly, Raz's whole argumentative strategy is begging the question: first he sets up by stipulation criteria for the law that do not include force (comprehensiveness, openness). In order to establish that force should not be included in the list of criteria, a situation is imagined in which force is supposedly absent. As I have argued above, force is not absent in this imagined situation. But even if it were, Raz argument would still not work: even if force were actually absent in the imagined situation, the question would still be if such a system counts as a legal system or not. Now Raz explicitly answers this question in

---

[54] B Rehfeldt, 'Recht, Religion und Moral bei den frühen Germanen' (1954) 71 *Zeitschrift der Savigny-Stiftung für Rechtsgeschichte. Germanische Abteilung* 1, 7–8.

the affirmative, but does so not by drawing on some independent argument, but simply by reference to the criteria, the completeness of which was contentious in the first place. So the 'thought experiment' solves the question of the completeness of criteria of law by assuming their completeness. But then what looks to be an argument, a thought experiment, turns out to be a long-winded stipulation. Force is thus excluded simply because it was not included in the first list of criteria. It is excluded only because it is excluded.

What Raz might have shown is that the imagined society might have a need for institutions that do determine conduct, decide individual cases, determine collective action, solve conflict and have formal decision procedures. But a local bridge club can do all of that. Not all institutions are legal. The local bridge club does not create law. Raz accepts that. When it comes to making clear what distinguishes the law from the rules of the local bridge club, he refers to comprehensiveness and openness. But, as I have argued above, in the particular way Raz frames comprehensiveness and openness, ie excluding effectiveness and force, a local bridge club could enact comprehensive and open rules.

4

Law as Permission

I. INTRODUCTION

URING MY TIME at various law schools in the United Kingdom, a popular question for the jurisprudence exam has been something along the following lines:

Can the law create obligations and, if so, how?

I think that this question has proven popular not only because it challenges the argumentative skills of the students, but also because some jurisprudence teachers themselves do not have a very satisfactory answer to that question and want to hear their students' opinions.

The question sends students and many jurisprudes alike into a kind of dizzying whirl: most want to argue that the law does, of course, create obligations. However, when queried as to how precisely the law does this, the answer appears increasingly elusive, until many give up and retract their original claim that the law actually creates obligations, at least in the original sense of the question.

The Pure Theory offers relief against this trouble. However, in order to see how the Pure Theory resolves this issue, one has to get an understanding of the aetiology of the problem. The difficulty in answering this question arises from a certain mental image that this question produces. According to this mental image, the law attempts to create obligations directly by obligating us. 'But how else would it try to create obligations?', one might ask, and since it sounds tautologically true that the law creates obligations by attempting to create obligations, one might struggle to even fathom the possibility of an alternative. That there is such an alternative and, what is more, an attractive one will be explored below. But let me further describe the assumptions of this mental image or model of the basic functioning of the law. According to the model, the law attempts to create obligations by demanding things from us, by claiming 'Do x!' or 'You ought to x'.

This mental image is, of course, closely tied up with the demand model described throughout this book. It assumes that the unproblematically given basic operation or ideal form of the law is to demand things from us.

In this chapter, I will introduce the alternative of the Pure Theory: that the basic operation of the law is not to *demand* things. Rather, demanding things can be explained in terms of a more basic operation, which is *allowing* things.

Note that the Pure Theory does not deny that the law is in the business of creating demands and obligations. However, it does deny that the law performs a normative standing jump and creates an obligation by simply demanding things. Rather, the Pure Theory argues that the law creates obligations by allowing things. Why should this solve anything? Well, the difference is this: whilst the transition from demanding something to something being 'objectively demanded' is normatively notoriously difficult, the transition from allowing something to something being 'objectively allowed' is not nearly as problematic. The move via permission thus allows us to tell an end story about the normativity of the law which the demand model does not yield. I will unpack this transition from allowing something to it being allowed in detail below.

Now, it is not a mere coincidence that the demand model has taken such a sway over jurisprudential thought. Its strength and intuitive appeal derives from the straightforward way in which it deals with the ordering function of the law. It has a neat story to tell about how the law orders society, how it remedies social ills and promotes goods. A demand quite neatly slots into the explanatory gaps here: if something is not as it ought to be, the law demands it to be different. However, this strength is more than outweighed by the difficulties it produces, namely its inability to satisfactorily answer the question of how making a demand can lead to there being an objective demand.

As I hope to be able to show, the strength of the permission model is that this transition is much less problematic. This benefit, however, does not come without cost: the difficulty for the permission model is to show how the world can be ordered simply by means of permissions. Whilst it is straightforwardly clear how the world is ordered by making use of demands, it is less apparent how permissions can be used to bring order to the world. This difficulty, however, is far from insurmountable, and is less of a substantive philosophical problem than a technical one: after all, the Pure Theory does not deny that the law makes demands and creates obligations. It only denies that the law makes demands by demanding things. It argues, conversely, that the law makes demands by allowing things. What needs to be shown, accordingly, is how demands can be made by allowing things, ie that demands can be analysed in terms of permissions.

Part of the task of the following chapter will be to reinterpret or reconstruct the ideal form of the law. Now, just as in the previous chapter, many might want to resist the attempt to even embark on the endeavour of such a reconstruction of the ideal form (or basic operation) of the law as it may seem artificial, distorting or simply an impossible task to perform. I have already dealt with a variant of this complaint in the previous chapter. So here it should suffice to say the following: people who resist an explicit reconstruction of the ideal form of the law are very often unaware that they themselves are operating from a conception of the ideal form of the law which needs to be reconstructed from the legal material. The primary rule 'No one ought to murder', for instance, can by no means be found immediately in the legal material itself. Rather, the legal material is a complex web of hypotheticals, cross-references, fictions, definitions and more, from which the legal mind reconstructs whatever it takes to be the basic operation.

The identification and reconstruction of the basic deontic operation of the law has to relate different expressions of the law and different forms of law to each other: ultimately we will identify obligation-creating norms of the form 'No one ought to murder' as secondary or derivative, and we will identify a permissive norms of the form 'The executive organ is allowed to execute a murderer' as primary or primitive. This is certainly a controversial result. To get used to this kind of argument, I will first present a rendering of a similar argument proffered by Stanley Paulson.

II. EMPOWERMENT

Stanley Paulson gave a somewhat similar analysis to the one I will present below in his reading of the work of Hans Kelsen. He argued that, according to Kelsen, 'empowering norms are fundamental, and what one has always fancied as deontic norms are nothing more than "constructions" built from a certain juxtaposition or "pairing" of empowering norms'.[1]

By 'deontic norms', Paulson is referring to norms that impose duties or create obligations, ie what I have called 'demands'. So, just like I will be arguing below, Paulson is arguing that what is usually treated as being primitive, namely the creation of obligations, is actually derivative and what is usually treated as derivative or secondary, namely the empowerment of agents, is actually primitive. One major difference between Paulson's claim and mine will be that whilst he finds the primitive deontic operator in *empowerment*, I will argue that we should better turn to *permission*. I will be arguing that only by turning to permission can we answer the big question that has been left open by the demand model.

In a sense, Paulson does not need to answer that big question as he is not in the business of arguing in favour of replacing one primitive deontic operator with another. Rather, he is in the business of interpreting Kelsen and

---

[1] SL Paulson, 'An Empowerment Theory of Legal Norms' (1988) 1 *Ratio Juris* 58, 60.

reconstructing what he thinks Kelsen argued. Still, as his discussion is both exceptionally clear and ambitious, it does help us get a feel for the logic of this reassessment of the primitive deontic operator of the law.

Paulson presents Kelsen as having gone through three stages in his assessment of the ideal form of legal norms: (i) the coupling theory; (ii) the eliminative theory; and (iii) the empowerment theory. For our purposes, only the last two theories are relevant.

According to Paulson, Kelsen, at various stages in his thoughts, presented what Paulson terms the 'eliminative theory'. According to Kelsen, this can be rendered along the following lines:

> I ought, or I am obligated, not to steal; I ought, or I am obligated, to repay a loan mean in the *positive* law *nothing other* than this: If I steal, I ought to be punished, if I fail to pay back a loan, a lien ought to be taken on my property.[2]

So, according to this theory, the norm 'No one ought to steal' is replaced or eliminated by the norm 'If someone steals, he ought to be punished'.

Whether or not calling this an 'elimination' is a good rendering of Kelsen's ideas is doubtful. After all, from a purely exegetical point of view, Kelsen does not himself use the term 'elimination' and, from a substantive point of view, we have to distinguish elimination from a claim of *explanatory primacy*. What Kelsen was rightly driving at was that a directive norm can be analysed in terms of an empowering norm and thus cannot enjoy explanatory primacy. Kelsen, for instance, tends to argue along the following lines:

> Modern criminal codes usually do not contain norms that prohibit, like the Ten Commandments, murder, adultery, and other crimes; they limit themselves to attach penal sanctions to certain behaviour. This shows clearly that a norm: 'You shall not murder' is superfluous, if a norm is valid: 'He who murders ought to be punished'.[3]

Here, all Kelsen is saying is that one norm is superfluous if another norm is valid. By 'superfluous', he certainly does not mean that the norm is not valid; rather, the opposite: it is valid even though it does not need to be posited itself. When the norm 'He who murders ought to be punished' is posited, then positing the norm 'You shall not murder' would be unnecessary. In legal systems, we actually do not posit this norm. This, however, does not mean that the norm is not valid. The norm itself is not eliminated; rather it is the need to posit it separately that is 'eliminated'.

Be that as it may, calling it eliminative or not, Paulson is certainly right that Kelsen reversed the explanatory relation between the norms 'You shall not

---

[2] H Kelsen, *Essays in Legal and Moral Philosophy*, ed O Weinberger, trans P Heath (Dordrecht, Reidel, 1973), 27–60, 32. Original emphasis.

[3] H Kelsen, *The Pure Theory of Law*, 2nd edn, trans M Knight (Berkeley, University of California Press, 1967) 55.

murder' and 'He who murders ought to be punished'. But Paulson also rightly observes that Kelsen has here replaced one duty-imposing norm with another duty-imposing one, ie one demand with another. One is directed at everyone and the other is directed at the officials. However, both make demands, both aim to create obligations.

This transition thus does not yet represent the full Kelsenian revolution. This will only be completed in the second step. Kelsen does this, according to Paulson, in what he calls the 'empowerment theory'. Paulson starts this line of argument by observing how Kelsen intends to extend the legal use of the term 'ought': '[Kelsen] now uses "ought" as akin to a variable expression, ranging over the specific modal expressions "should" or "must," "may," and "can," marking commanding, permissory, and empowering norms respectively'.[4] Whether the term 'ought' should, or whether it even can, be used in this extended form is itself open to debate. However, Kelsen is certainly right that, just as we have more than one alethic modality (next to necessity we also have possibility, contingency and impossibility), we also have more than one normative modality (next to prescription we have permission, indifference and proscription). It seems that he proposes to use the term 'ought' as a *pars pro toto* label for normative modality as such.

This widening of the repertoire of normative modalities, however, poses the following question: which of the three deontic operators correctly instantiates in the second 'ought' in the elimination theory? The 'ought not' of the eliminated norm 'You *ought not* to kill' certainly means 'must not' or 'should not'. But what about the 'ought' in the more fundamental norm, 'If you kill, a person *ought* to apply sanction to you'? Does this necessary mean 'should' or 'must'?

Kelsen's own answer is quite clear:

> The official's imposition of a sanction is commanded, has the content of a legal obligation, if its omission is understood in turn as the condition of a sanction. But where this is not the case then the official is simply empowered to impose the sanction, not commanded.[5]

So, according to Kelsen, the 'ought' directed at the official can be resolved either into a 'must' in the traditional sense of ought or into a 'can' in the sense of an empowerment. Note at this stage that Kelsen and Paulson do not contemplate the possibility of the 'may', ie the permission, taking the role of the deontic operator in terms of which the others are analysed.

---

[4] Paulson (n 1) 67. See also J Raz, *The Concept of a Legal System. An Introduction to the Theory of Legal System* (Oxford, Clarendon, 1997), 47.

[5] Kelsen (n 3) 25.

The following question then arises: if the 'ought' directed at the official can be resolved into two different deontic operators, is there a relation between these two? Is one primary? Are they sitting unrelated next to each other? Now, Paulson resolves this as follows: if we understand the ought of the norm directed against the official as 'must' or 'should', we would be sent into an infinite regress where the meaning of one ought would explained by another 'ought'. This regress can only come to an end if and in so far as we understand the ought directed at the official as empowering him to apply the sanction. This, however, makes rendering the ought directed at the official as empowering the official more basic than rendering it as obligating him.

Paulson calls resolving the ought in terms of 'must' or 'ought' the *strong interpretation* and resolving it in terms of 'can' the *weak interpretation*, and concludes that Kelsen

> is saying that the strong interpretation is simply a construction built out of the weak one, and that the empowerment modality of the weak interpretation is the key to both … But in both cases the operative modality is that of empowerment, with the 'command'-talk representing a particular construction out of the empowerment modality.[6]

So, according to Paulson's reading of Kelsen, all commands of a legal system can be traced back to the following norm:

— If citizen C fails to do x, then a certain legal official A is empowered to impose a certain sanction y on C.

The problems with both the 'elimination theory' and the 'empowerment theory' are well known, have been extensively discussed in the literature and can be mapped out along the following three axes: (i) the infinite regress argument, (ii) the non-coerced obligations argument; and (iii) implausibility argument.

(i) The infinite regress argument challenges the whole strategy of explaining one obligation in terms of another by arguing that this leads to an infinite regress: if we analyse obligation in terms of another obligation, we face the dilemma that we will either never come to an end or come up against an obligation which remains unanalysed. Neither of these two options is viable as both leave the entire chain of obligations unexplained. Paulson thinks that Kelsen takes care of the regress argument by means of his empowerment theory. Surely, if the first obligation is in need of explanation and we ultimately explain it in terms of an empowerment, then we have achieved at least something? However, we have not really halted the regress. After all, why should empowerment not itself be in need of explanation? Neither Paulson nor Kelsen offers a solution here. Neither tells a story of how and why

---

[6] Paulson (n 1) 69.

empowerment is indeed primitive in the sense of not needing or not being open to further analysis. However, such a story—an end story, so to speak—needs to be told. I will attempt to do that by explaining how only permission can function as a keystone completing the argumentative edifice. I think that, ultimately, only the theory presented below can avoid the worry of the infinite regress.

(ii) The non-coerced or naked obligation argument has become a staple argument against the Pure Theory and many believe that it is fatal for the latter. Hart, for instance, argues that in every legal system there are obligations which cannot be analysed in terms of obligations directed at other organs as these obligations are bona fide obligations, such as the obligation of a legal organ to apply the law. Now, this line of criticism differs from the infinite regress argument as it claims that those kinds of obligations not only emerge at the extremes of the legal system, ie where the last official is called to take coercive actions, but occur everywhere throughout the legal hierarchy. The obligation of officials to apply the law, it is argued, is just a naked obligation with no empowerment or permission of the use of force attached. Officials simply have a primitive obligation to apply the law. This, it is argued, immediately renders futile any attempt to show that all legal obligations can be analysed in terms of other deontic operators, be it empowerment or permission.

I think this argument is mistaken: to start with, officials do certainly have duties that are analysable in terms of the empowerment of other officials. If a policeman disobeys the commands of his superior in applying the law, he opens himself up to the possibility of disciplinary proceedings. Similarly, judges who act in gross violation of their duties may also face disciplinary charges. However, these latter duties are not the duties to which the above line of criticism refers. The obligations referred to as naked by this argument are not administrative duties or duties that emerge from employment or court organisation. Of course, if a judge does not show up for work, he can be disciplined. But is there not a sense that judges have a general duty to apply the law that goes beyond the judge's administrative duty to do his job?

Well, no. To illustrate the point, let us have a look at another 'official': Parliament (or a single member thereof) certainly does not have a duty imposed by the constitution to create a certain law. Rather, it is empowered or authorised by the constitution to create statutes. In a similar sense, the judge does not have a duty to apply the law, but has authority or power to do so. He will certainly have motives to apply the law correctly: he might want to get ahead in his job, he might like the social prestige or he might simply enjoy putting people into prison. Now, the law allows that some of his externally motivated judgments become law. Conversely, if I simply enjoyed putting people into prison, my request to incarcerate someone would certainly not count as a valid court judgment, even if the person concerned is clearly guilty of the crime.

I and the judge might have the same motives for requesting someone's incarcerations and the same material justification for putting the person away. The difference is that the law authorises or empowers him, whereas it does not authorise or empower me. The judge first and foremost has a power which allows him to put people in prison. So the judge has (extra-legal) motives to apply the law and legal authority to apply the law. Is there anything missing in this picture? Does he have a legal duty to put people in prison, or a general duty to apply the law that goes beyond both his legal authority and the general job-related duties he has as a judge? To argue that this is the case would be odd: after all, legally the judge can only do what the law authorises him to do. The judge thus cannot do what the law does not allow him to do. He cannot create unlawful law. He is, by definition, not empowered to do so.[7] It would thus be an odd duty for him to not do something which he is incapable of doing in the first place. So the judge does not have a legal duty to apply the law; rather, just as in case of Parliament, he has legal authority to do certain things which he needs extra-legal motivation to do.

Those naked legal obligations thus do not exist. Furthermore, they do not serve any theoretical purpose, ie we do not need them to exist: motivation plus the authorisation by the law provides all we need to know to understand the working of a legal system.

(iii) The implausibility argument is certainly the most powerful one in Hart's arsenal. He argues that the entire elimination manoeuvre leads to forced conclusions and that the 'inversion of ancillary and principal'[8] is highly implausible. In order to demonstrate this, Hart offers a positive and a negative argument: first, he proffers a broad methodological claim about the point of jurisprudence; secondly, he presents a *reductio ad absurdum* of the elimination theory.

The sweeping methodological claim consists in arguing, in Leslie Green's rendering, that

> there is no essentialist, 'metaphysical', answer to the question of how to divide up legal material into individual laws; the best approach is one that lets us understand law as it is for those who actually use it, most of whom live outside courtrooms.[9]

---

[7] The can of worms that is opened by this rather obvious insight, which is a necessary and simply truth, namely, that there is no unlawful law and that, in so far as there is annullable law, there has to be a legal norm that renders this to-be-annulled law at least provisionally lawful, is dealt with by the important doctrine of the so-called *Fehlerkalkül* or alternative authorisation. See C Kletzer, 'Kelsen's Development of the *Fehlerkalkül*-Theory' (2005) 18 *Ratio Juris* 46; L Vinx, *Kelsen's Pure Theory of Law. Legality and Legitimacy* (Oxford, Oxford University Press, 2007) ch 3.

[8] HLA Hart, *The Concept of Law*, 2nd edn (Oxford, Oxford University Press, 1994), 40.

[9] L Green, 'Introduction' in HLA Hart, *The Concept of Law*, 3rd edn (Oxford, Oxford University Press, 2012) xv–lv, xxxii.

The claim is based on the idea that

> the principal functions of the law as a means of social control are not to be seen in private litigation or prosecutions, which represent vital but still ancillary provisions for the failures of the system. It is to be seen in the diverse ways in which the law is used to control, to guide, and to plan life out of court.[10]

To start with, this is patently begging the question of why this should be so. The issue nevertheless remains that the Pure Theory is not denying that the law might be mainly in the business of controlling, guiding and planning life. What the Pure Theory claims is that the law controls, guides and plans life outside of the courts by means of empowering (or allowing) the use of force. The law regulates life outside of the courtroom—say, my everyday behaviour—by means of holding out the prospect of me being subjected to brute force. Hart himself accepts that in what Raz has called a 'Kelsenian twist'.[11]

Now, the Hartian will retort that no philosophical insight is gained when the philosophical position diverges from the position of our everyday use of words. I do not think that this is a convincing argument. Apart from presenting a rather meek image of philosophy, it is not clear why the question of how the law does what it does should be a purely common-sense question and not a highly technical one. Imagine that a 'Kelsenian' physiologist argued that the heart transports blood by means of muscular contraction and a 'Hartian' physiologist countered that it is absurd to think along those lines as everybody knows that the function of the heart is to pump blood. We would think that the 'Hartian' misunderstood the issue.

Now for the *reductio*: Hart argues that, according to the logic of the empowerment theory, one could argue that in a game of sport, too, all rules 'are *really* rules directing officials to do certain things under certain conditions'.[12] In this line of argument, all depends on the word 'really'. As we have seen, the Pure Theory of Law does indeed argue that demands are superfluous given a permission to use force. It also argues that, since the reverse is not true, the permission of force is primitive or basic. What the Pure Theory does not argue, however, is that there are no secondary legal rules demanding things from people or that people would misunderstand the law if they took it to demand something from them. However, the example only leads to an absurd result if we supposed this latter reading. Since this latter reading is not what the Pure Theory claims, the attack comes to nothing.

What the Pure Theory claims is only that *if* there is a rule, say, allowing a referee to award a penalty if the ball was played with the hand, then the rule

---

[10] Hart, *Concept of Law* (n 8) 40.

[11] HLA Hart, *Essays on Bentham. Jurisprudence and Political Theory* (Oxford, Oxford University Press, 1982) 160; J Raz, 'Hart on Moral Rights and Legal Duties' (1984) 4 *OJLS* 123, 131.

[12] Hart, *Concept of Law*, 40. Original emphasis.

that the ball must not be played with the hand would be superfluous, and that *if* there was a rule demanding that players must not play the ball with the hand, then such a rule would *not* make a rule allowing a referee to award a penalty superfluous, thus rendering the rule directed at the referee more basic. The Pure Theory is not in the business of claiming which of those rules will or should be part of the rulebook, or how a player should understand a rule.

III. PERMISSION

Paulson is, I think, correct in his attribution of the argument to Kelsen and also roughly on the right track in the argument itself. However, I think that Kelsen himself was not entirely on point. After all, why should we think that the primitive normative function should be sought in empowerment? Empowerment means the conferral of a power on someone to change the normative status of someone else, in particular the power to enact norms. This is at least as complex and puzzling a normative notion as obligation is. Why should we think we have gained anything if we have explained obligation in terms of empowerment? Have we not committed the fallacy of explaining *obscurum per obscurius*?

What is more, it is unclear how empowerment actually fits the cases we have before us: in what sense should we speak of the law 'empowering' someone to enact a sanction? This seems odd. It would only make sense if the sanction could be understood as an individual norm which is immediately applied at the same time of its enactment. This, however, seems overly complicated.

So, whilst Paulson was on the right track, I think he floundered just before the finishing line. He is correct in demanding an inquiry into the ideal or primitive form of legal norms. What he did not get right was which deontic operator features in this ideal or primitive form. As I will argue below, it should be permission and not empowerment. This means that, according to the Pure Theory, the Paulsonian ideal form

> If citizen C fails to do x, then a certain legal official A is empowered to impose a certain sanction y on C.

will be replaced by the following:

> If A does X, then someone else is allowed to use force against A.

The centrality of the use of force has been discussed in the previous chapter. Here, I will not focus on the object of permission, but on the permission itself. I want to make clear why I think that only permission can possibly play the role of helping us tell the end story of the law, ie completing the story of how exactly the law can create obligations. This story will illustrate how the law as a very specific social technique exploits a normative peculiarity of permissions. The following chapter is dedicated to illustrating this peculiarity.

If the following remarks sound too speculative to some, let me present two brief remarks in my defence: first, any end story will have a certain dialectic nature to it, and avoiding such dialectics will very often be only possible at the cost of superficiality; secondly, my claims about permissions are not meant to be presenting a final, conclusive rendering of a comprehensive theory of permissions. Rather I want to highlight a couple of important and decisive features of permissions which I think are essential to explaining how the law goes about creating obligations and which have not been picked up in the literature.

In jurisprudence, *obligation* and *prohibition* are regularly treated as the paradigmatic normative operators, whereas *permission* is taken to be secondary or subsidiary.[13] Paulson's arguments introduced above suggest that this might be a mistake: rather than explaining permission in terms of obligation, it might be more rewarding to explain obligation in terms of permission. As illustrated in chapter three, the obligation not to kill someone might be parasitic on the permission to kill someone who has killed another.

This focus on permission is not entirely unprecedented. As, for instance, Tierney worked out in quite some detail, permissive law has played an important role in European legal thinking since at least the era of Roman law. Most of that discourse focused on the question of whether human law might permit actions which were forbidden by natural law: 'The most important feature of permissive human law that distinguished it from natural permissive law was that human law could and often did tolerate actions that were considered illicit in themselves or contrary to natural moral law.'[14] In the Middle Ages, the issue of permissive laws arose mostly within the context of prostitution, usury and the practice of non-Christian rites. The perception was that, despite the fact that these acts were clearly contrary to natural law, prohibiting them would cause greater harm than good.[15] Thus, Aquinas, for instance, claimed that a human permissive law should allow certain vices that did not harm the common good.[16] Kant also wrote that a *lex permissiva* as a human law 'condones what natural law condemns'.[17]

---

[13] Permission is taken to be 'subsidiary'. See N Bobbio, 'Norma' in *Enciclopedia Einaudi*, vol 9 (Turin, Einaudi, 1980) 891–2; E Bulygin, 'Permissive Norms and Normative Systems' in A Martino and F Socci-Natali (eds), *Automated Analysis of Legal Texts* (Amsterdam, Elsevier Science, 1986) 216; J Raz, *Practical Reason and Norms* (Oxford, Oxford University Press, 1999) 50; Raz (n 4) 121.

[14] B Tierney, 'Permissive Natural Law and Property: Gratian to Kant' (2001) 62 *Journal of the History of Ideas* 381, 387.

[15] I Bejczy, 'Tolerantia: A Medieval Concept' (1997) 58 *Journal of the History of Ideas* 365, 371; A Brundage, 'Prostitution in Medieval Canon Law' in V Bullough and Brundage (eds), *Sexual Practices and the Medieval Church* (Buffalo, Prometheus Books, 1982) 149–60.

[16] Aquinas, Summa theologiae, 2.2ae.10.11 and 1.2ae.96.3. See Tierney (n 14) 387.

[17] I Kant, 'Kant on the Metaphysics of Morals: Vigilantius's Lecture Notes' in P Heath and JB Schneewind (eds), *The Cambridge Edition of the Works of Immanuel Kant. Lectures on Ethics* (Cambridge, 1997) 280 (XXVII, 516).

But permissive laws have also played a central role in classic theories of property. On the face of it, private possession can seem contrary to natural law: private property has its origin outside of the civil state. So how can we explain that, outside of a civil state, my unilateral will can create obligations in others? The solution to this classic quandary has very often been a permissive principle within natural law itself.[18]

It was Fichte, who we identified as the forebear of the Pure Theory, who put this permissive law at centre stage of legal philosophy:

> A right is something that one can avail oneself of or not. Thus a right follows from a merely permissive law, and it is a permissive law because it is limited only to a certain sphere, from which it can be inferred that outside the sphere of the law one is free from it, and if there is no other law concerning the object, one is generally left solely to one's own arbitrary will. This permission is not explicitly contained in the law; it is merely inferred from an interpretation of the law, from its limited character. The limited character of law manifests itself in the fact that it is conditioned. It is absolutely impossible to see how a permissive law should be derivable from the moral law, which commands unconditionally and thereby extends its reach to everything.[19]

For Fichte, this *absolute impossibility* to see how a permissive law should be derivable from the moral law also settles the relation of law and morality. He thus believed that the law has to find its basis somewhere other than in morality. This also determines Fichte's understanding of the specific crux of legal philosophy: 'How is it possible for a law to command by not commanding?'[20] If the law is basically permissive, how does it create obligations? If it consists mainly in issuing permissions, why does it look so differently on the surface of it? These questions are, for Fichte, the same as the following questions: 'How can the law have force by not being in force?' and 'How can the law encompass a sphere by not encompassing it?'[21] What Fichte is referring to here is exactly the relation between the law creating obligations and it permitting the use of force. Fichte writes:

> The answer is: all this necessarily follows if the law prescribes a determinate sphere for itself, if it directly carries within itself the quantity of its own validity. As soon as the law indicates the sphere to which it applies, it thereby simultaneously determines the sphere to which it does not apply; it explicitly holds itself back from anything about this sphere and making prescriptions with respect to it.—In relation to

---

[18] Tierney (n 14).
[19] JG Fichte, *Foundations of Natural Right*, ed F Neuhouser, trans M Baur (Cambridge, Cambridge University Press, 2000) 14.
[20] ibid 83.
[21] ibid.

a particular person, I am absolved from adhering to the law requiring me to treat him as a free being, and the question of how I will treat him depends solely upon my free choice, or I have a right of coercion against him. These claims mean, and can mean, nothing other than: this person cannot, through the law of right alone, prevent my coercion of him (although he may well do so through other laws, by physical strength, or by appealing to the moral law). My coercion is not contrary to this law, and if the other person has nothing to appeal to by it, he must endure my coercion of him.[22]

This is a very clear rendering of precisely the relation we are after in our attempt to understand the Pure Theory's analysis of legal obligation: all the law needs to do in order to be law is 'to indicate the sphere to which it applies'. By that, the law has 'simultaneously indicated a sphere to which it does not apply'. It has thus indicated a sphere where everyone is legally free to do what he wants. This legal freedom includes the permission to use force. Similarly, as we have seen above in chapter three, section III, the law permits the use of force by declaring that it has no legal consequences.

IV. THE NATURALISTIC LOGIC OF PERMISSION

Permissions are strange normative creatures. In one sense, they are very weak normative operators: permissions do not bind us in the way than obligations or prohibitions do. They leave room for choice. They open up routes of actions and do not close them down. This weakness of permissions is, I think, why their central importance has been largely overlooked in recent debates in philosophy of law.

In at least two other senses, permissions are very potent normative operators. First, permissions are irresistible and inviolable: whereas I can resist or violate a prohibition by doing or attempting to do what is forbidden, I cannot resist or violate a permission. If someone allows me to take his pudding, I can do nothing to counter that permission. I can take the pudding or leave it; both are within the scope of the permission. This irresistibility holds irrespective of whether the permission is valid or not. If it is invalid, I can, of course, argue with it, but there is no immediate action I could take in order to resist or violate it. If someone allowed me to kill my grandmother, I cannot resist this permission. I can argue with it, but neither killing my grandmother nor not killing her would constitute resistance against or a violation of that invalid permission. Conversely, if someone forbids me to eat my own pudding, I do not need to argue; I can simply resist or violate this invalid prohibition by eating my own pudding.

---

[22] ibid.

Besides this irresistibility and inviolability there is a second, related sense in which permissions are potent normative operators: permissions enjoy a discursive immunity vis-à-vis radical or nihilistic criticisms of morality. In order to illustrate this odd feature of permissions, we can again compare them with obligations and prohibitions which do not share this property. Let us assume that you claim that I have an obligation to help the poor. If I criticised your claim, arguing (a_o) that from the moral standards we both share no such duty can be derived, and if I were to convince you, then we would agree that there is no obligation of that specific kind. If I strengthened my claim, arguing (b_o) that under no moral standard there is such a duty, and if I convinced you, then we would agree that there is no such obligation. If I further pushed the criticism beyond the threshold of moral scepticism and argued (c_o) that there is no such duty because there is no morality at all, that there are no moral truths out there, and I were to convince you, then, again, the result would be that there would be no obligation to help the poor. This is all straightforward.

The result is different in the case of permissions. Let us say you claim that you are permitted to take from the rich what is needed to help the poor. Now, if I criticised your claim, arguing (a_p) that under our shared moral standard there is no such permission, and if I were to convince you, then we would agree that there is no such permission. If I strengthened my claim, arguing (b_p) that under no moral standard there is such a permission, and if I were to convince you, then we would agree that there is no such permission. However, if I further pushed the criticism beyond the threshold of moral scepticism and argued (c_p) that there is no morality, that there are no objective moral truths out there, then the result would be radically different: in this case, nothing would be obligatory, nothing would be prohibited. It would thus also not be the case that you are prohibited from taking from the rich and giving to the poor. You would thus be permitted to do anything you like, including taking what you claim you need from the rich. That this permission is what is called a 'weak' permission does not matter, since, as I will concur with Raz below, there is no meaningful distinction between strong and weak permissions. The result is but the nihilistic 'everything is permitted' that we know from Dostoyevsky.[23]

There is thus an odd discontinuity in relation to the moral scrutiny of permission. Whereas prohibitions and prescriptions are fully susceptible to doubt, permissions are open only to partial doubt. Put reversely: when a criticism against a certain permission is made more radical, the radicalised version of the criticism helps to reinstate the permission rather than undermine it.

---

[23] F Dostoyevsky, *The Brothers Karamazov* (London, Penguin, 2003) ch 5.

But does this not blur the distinction between strong and weak permissions? Is it not so that cases a_p and b_p were concerned with a strong permission, ie an exceptional permission that is meant to defeat a general duty, whereas what results in case c_p is merely a weak permission, ie a general permission, which is the mere obverse of the absence of any obligation? The distinction between weak and strong permissions is not as clear cut as one might think. According to Raz, 'the distinction between permissions granted by an enacted norm and other permissions does not seem to lead anywhere'. In order to demonstrate this, he argues that it is impossible to decide which of the following statements are strong permissions and which are not:[24]

(a) Every x ought to φ in C.
(b) Everybody ought to φ in C except one who is not an x.
(c) Everyone ought to φ in C and everyone who is not an x is permitted not to φ in C.

Since all depends on the formulation of the permission and not on the permission itself, there is no decision procedure to sift out strong permissions from weak ones.

> Does anything turn on whether an obligation is imposed on people over thirty or on all with an exception for those under thirty? Are we to say that if the law is formulated in the first way then those under thirty have a weak permission to refrain from the action required of their elders, whereas if it is formulated in the second way they have a strong permission? ... It seems to me that the distinction between strong and weak permissions as it is commonly drawn makes little sense ... In the final analysis strong and weak permissions are permissions in precisely the same sense differing only in their source ... It is partly because no substantive distinction between strong and weak permissions has been established, that it is difficult to know which law establishes a strong permission and which does not. Since there is no difference in normative force of the permissions one is forced, in order to draw the distinction, to rely on linguistic and formalistic criteria lacking any rationale.[25]

In precisely that vein—namely, that there is no difference in normative force between strong and weak permissions—radical criticism, if true, leads to the situation where no one can meaningfully claim that the act in question is prohibited. This means that no one can meaningfully counter me if I claim that it is permitted. Rather than weakening the argument, the distinction between weak and strong permissions in fact simply restates the odd discontinuity within permissions. In the case of obligations, such a duality does not exist. There is no parallel sense in which we have weak obligations as opposed to strong obligations.

---

[24] Raz, *Practical Reason* (n 13) 87.
[25] ibid 88.

So the normative strength of permissions rests in the peculiar fact that, structurally, permissions can be seen as placeholders of moral scepticism or normative nihilism within normativity itself. Permissions are immune to the challenges of moral scepticism: if moral scepticism is true, then there is no obligation to do anything. This, however, means that we are permitted to do anything. So, in issuing permissions, one can rely on either of two opposites: on normative convictions or on the absence of normative convictions. The same is not true for obligations and prohibitions.

Why should this odd robustness matter? Take a look at the following two factual (a, b) and two normative (α, β) statements:

(a)   Someone ordered me to give him my pudding.
(b)   Someone allowed me to take his pudding.
(α)   Giving him my pudding is obligatory.
(β)   Taking his pudding is permitted.

One classic puzzle of jurisprudence is to understand the transition from factual statements of the kind of (a) to normative statements of the kind of (α), ie to understand how the fact that someone has issued an order can lead to a situation where I really am under an obligation. Put in terms of the Pure Theory, the problem is to see how the subjective meaning of an act of will can also be its objective meaning.

When someone orders me to give him my pudding, this does not by itself tell me very much, certainly not enough to know whether I really am under an obligation. It remains an open question whether I really am under an obligation to give him my pudding, because this depends on whether this someone has the authority or competence to order me to give him my pudding. Now, whether his supposed authority ensues from a higher norm (a police officer confiscates my pudding following criminal procedures), from a service the issuer of the order is supposed to provide to me by issuing the order (a doctor aware of my fatal diabetes tells me to hand over the deadly sweet), from an actual or hypothetical contract I have entered into with the issuer of the order (the sovereign of Britain tells me to hand over the pudding), from a non-contractual role I play in an association with the issuer of the order (my mother tells me to stop eating pudding at my age) or from whatever else, it should be clear that something else other than the order itself has to do the job of justifying the transition from the fact of an order being issued to there actually being an obligation. So, in case of an order, the order cannot itself tell me that it is binding. A demand cannot qua demand possibly feature in an end story about the normativity of the law. After all, any story we tell that justifies the binding-ness of the order is itself open to being queried about its own justification.

But why is it the case that we need a justification in order to interpret the subjective meaning of a prescriptive utterance as being its objective meaning?

We need such a justification because of the distribution of the burden of proof. If someone claims that an obligation exists, the burden is on him to demonstrate that. Why is this so? It is because being under an obligation is not the default normative state of actual affairs. The world as it is is not in a deontological tilt, it is level.[26] This is not meant to express a profound metaphysical or ontological insight, but is simply the necessary truth that if we leave aside all normative facts or reasons that could be given, there are no normative facts or reasons left and thus what remains is a morally inert world. Such an operation of abstracting from everything normative does, in a sense, depend on our capability to distinguish between the normative and the factual, between the word as it is and the word as it ought to be. I write 'in a sense' because I will try to show below that it does not totally depend on this distinction and in fact ends up undermining the distinction. However, I think that this distinction at this level is not controversial. Rather, if someone claimed that, apart from borderline cases, this distinction is impossible, such a claim would suffer a fatal inherent inconsistency: we can only understand what it means that the world ought to be something if we can distinguish what the world ought to be from what it actually is.

This is, I think, stating the obvious. It is stating that there are no 'weak obligations' which would be analogous to weak permissions, which would apply simply by virtue of the absence of a permission: the stone in front of me is grey, it has a certain form and a certain weight, but it is certainly not under an obligation to either be grey or not be grey. It does not owe anything to anyone and thus there is no sense in which it ought ('owed') to do or be anything. Now, because being under an obligation is not the default normative state, we need to be 'put' under an obligation, which, in turn, requires a justification, an explanation. An obligation does not explain itself.[27]

---

[26] I do not think that a refutation of this can be drawn from Geach's argument that words cannot simply shift in meaning when we move from one premise to the other in a syllogism. Even if it followed from Geach's argument that in order to be consistent we have to be able to accommodate moral facts in our logical and common language calculus, it does not follow that these facts are not fundamentally different from non-moral or natural facts. They might be best described as 'quasi-facts'. Jaap Hage seems to try to use Geach's argument to establish the existence of moral facts. J Hage, 'Separating Rules from Normativity' in M Araszkiewicz et al (eds), *Problems of Normativity, Rules and Rule-Following* (Cham, Springer, 2015) 19; PT Geach, 'Assertion' (1965) 74 *The Philosophical Review* 449. For an account of quasi-realism see S Blackburn, *Essays in Quasi-Realism* (Oxford, Oxford University Press, 1993).

[27] Now, all of these are in a sense 'theoretical' and not practical statements. They are not the result of any meta-ethical commitment and apply irrespective of whether we were to hold realist, anti-realist, cognitivist or non-cognitivist convictions. Rather, they state that, whatever your meta-ethical commitment, if you abstracted from your moral view and viewed the world entirely theoretically, what would remain, obviously or even per definition, would be a morally inert world. So all that is claimed is that, in terms of theoretical philosophy, we are not under an obligation to do anything (since there is no default theoretical obligation that binds us); all that

So, whilst not aiming to be a metaphysical claim, it is easy to see how the reverse claim, ie the claim that our default normative state is being under an obligation, would indeed be a profound metaphysical claim. It should thus come as no surprise that within theological systems human existence can be determined as a state of 'being under obligation', as, for instance, the Christian doctrine of the original sin might indicate. And, of course, a legal philosophy that starts from the normative premise that the world owes something to God will reach fundamentally different results than a jurisprudence that starts from the premise that the world (including man) does not *ex ante* owe anything to anyone but is in principle allowed to be as it is. The former will see no problem in obligation. This swift establishment of obligation, however, comes at the theoretically unbearable cost of having introduced a strange entity, that of a divine lawgiver. We can thus, following Anscombe, reverse the charge: if someone succeeds in establishing a full and unproblematic legal obligation, this is a strong indicator that there is somewhere hidden either a divine legislator or at least his long shadow: after all,

> those who recognise the origins of the notions of 'obligation' and of the emphatic, 'moral', ought, in the divine law conception of ethics, but who reject the notion of a divine legislator, sometimes look about for the possibility of retaining a law conception without a divine legislator.[28]

In modern secular, scientific, liberal states and in a legal philosophy that tries to understand not divine law but human law, the default normative state of the world has to be that the world is permitted to be what it is.[29] This, in turn, makes obligation problematic.

All of this leads to the following conclusion: the default normative state of us as natural beings is 'not being under an obligation'; this natural state, however, is still a normative state, or it finds its correspondence in normative language; it could also be described a 'being permitted to everything'. Raz puts it as follows: 'A person is permitted to perform an action if, and only if, it is not the case that he ought, all things considered, to refrain from it.'[30]

---

is stated is that if we were perfect moral sceptics, what would remain would be a morally inert, plain world of morally neutral facts. I am therefore not claiming that we actually all are or should be such perfect moral sceptics. Practically speaking, we might, of course, be under very stringent obligations, and those obligations are the subject matter of moral philosophy. Kant, for instance, tried to show in the Groundwork that whereas nature as reconstructed by natural sciences is normatively inert, being human, ie being a 'limited rational being', means putting oneself under certain obligations. So I am not denying that there are moral obligations, all I am denying is that all facts are by themselves moral facts that can be understood in terms of obligations.

[28] GEM Anscombe, 'Modern Moral Philosophy' (1958) 33 *Philosophy* 1.

[29] Again, this does not exclude moral or prudential action, since being permitted to be what it is, is only the default normative state and not the ultimate normative state.

[30] Raz, *Practical Reason* (n 13) 85.

On the grand scale, this means that the world may be everything, as there is no pregiven obligation. Since we are part of 'the world', our default normative state is to be permitted to be and to do everything.

So any permission can be based either on a substantive moral theory, such as Kantianism or utilitarianism, or, as a universal back-up, on a radically naturalistic moral theory according to which everything is permitted. For permissions, there is always the possibility to ground them in a radical Spinozism, according to which any legal permission extends just as far as one's power extends:

> For it is certain that nature, considered wholly in itself, has a sovereign right to do everything that it can do, ie, the right of nature extends as far as its power extends ... it follows that each individual thing has the sovereign right to do everything that it can do, or the right of each thing extends so far as its determined power extends.[31]

This, however, means the following:

> Anyone therefore deemed to be under the government of nature alone is permitted by the sovereign right of nature to desire anything that he believes to be useful to himself, whether brought to this by sound reason or by the impulse of his passions. He is permitted to take it for himself by any means—by force, by fraud, by pleading—whatever will most easily enable him to obtain it, and thus he is permitted to regard as an enemy anyone who tries to prevent his getting his way. From this it follows that the right, and the order of nature, under which all human beings are born and for the most part live, prohibits nothing but what no one desires or no one can do.[32]

This is the Spinozist baseline argument or fall-back option on which any permission can always be based. It represents a rather sober and hard-nosed naturalism that simply denies than man inhabits an *imperium in imperio*, a state within a state, and demands that man, in understanding his own affairs, does not pretend to be living outside nature and does not pretend that he is subject to completely different laws and principles than the one he applies when studying nature:

> Yet most people ... think of men in Nature as a state within a state (*imperium in imperio*). They hold that the human mind is not produced by natural causes but is directly created by God and is so independent of other things, that it has an absolute power to determine itself and to use reason in a correct way.[33]

---

[31] B De Spinoza, *Theological-Political Treatise*, trans M Silverthrone and J Israel (Cambridge, Cambridge University Press, 2007) 195.

[32] ibid 196–97.

[33] B De Spinoza, *Complete Works*, trans S Shirley (Cambridge, Hackett, 2002) 684.

Now, I am here not defending such a radical naturalism, ie I am not claiming that Spinoza is right and that there is indeed such a basic licence which is coextensive to one's powers. All I am arguing is that if we wanted to undermine a permission and thus subjected it to rational criticism, this radical criticism, if followed through to its logical conclusion, would reinstate the permission rather than undermine it. So one need not be committed to such a naturalism to see that it looms at the other side of whatever moral outlook one takes. And since permissions can be based either in this moral outlook or on its opposite, they provide a special robustness capable of delivering the required end story.

To summarise this end story: we have seen that the transition from subjective to objective obligation needs authoritative grounding because obligation is not our default normative state. If, however, it is the case that 'being permitted' is the default normative state of human existence, and if the transition from the subjective to the objective meaning of normative utterances only poses a problem for normative claims that depart from the default normative state, then the objective validity of permissions is in principle unproblematic. As opposed to obligations and prohibitions, permissions are not valid by grace of something else, but they are, in a sense, valid in themselves.

V. THE FUNCTIONING OF PERMISSIONS

Permissions are thus normatively more complete than orders or prohibitions. However, they are technically unwieldy. Orders and prohibitions are technically wieldy but are normatively incomplete. By using orders and prohibitions, it might be easy to organise people, but the legitimacy of that organisation is always inherently doubtful. Other, external goals or higher obligations are always needed to ground the validity of a normative system based on orders or prohibitions.

Now, since it seems impossible to make orders complete, it might be better to make permissions technically operative. This is precisely what positive law does. The positive law can be understood as the historically sustained attempt to make permissions technically operative. It is the attempt to use permissions in such a way as to organise society. It has taken the history of mankind to find ways to bring together the normative self-containment of permission with the technical operability of orders. This is done quite straightforwardly by ordering by means of permissions. Instead of simply ordering A to abstain from, say, desecrating churches, and then not being able to explain how this order can ever create an obligation, the law had been solving this problem for millennia by not directly ordering A to abstain from anything but by permitting the use of force or violence against A if he should desecrate a church. Now this permission is both philosophically and practically less problematic than an order. Nevertheless, the obligation of A not to desecrate churches is based on this permission.

How is it so? Take the norm introduced in the previous chapter:

(3)   Killing someone who has killed someone else unlawfully is lawful.

This norm will prestructure the reasoning of agents. If the agents are reasonable, considering the primary norm (3) above will make them say to themselves: (a) 'I ought not to kill another member'. This, however, means: (b) 'If I do not want a killing of me to be lawful, I ought not to kill another member'.

Norm (a) is a 'tertiary' norm and norm (b) is a 'secondary' norm. These norms are vested with only hypothetical normativity. Their bindingness depends on the motivation and beliefs of the agents.

Only the primary norms possess more than hypothetical normativity. The primary norm (3) is valid independently of the beliefs and motives of the agents. It applies categorically.

Even though this normativity is categorical, it is still oblique. It neither prescribes nor forbids anything. It just states that the killing of a killer is lawful and thus allowed. The *legal* obligation not to kill based on this permission is thus not a *moral* obligation. Whilst there is, of course, a moral obligation not to kill that is independent from the legal obligation, the legal obligation not to kill that rests on the permission to kill the killer is different from that moral obligation. Nor is it merely prudential: it is not based merely on the end of wanting to avoid the actual use of force. It is based, rather, on the end of wanting to avoid the legal status that the use of force against one would be lawful or permitted. Thus, whilst being hypothetical, the legal ought is not merely prudential.

This is so because the law at its basic level does not issue a threat. A threat aims at merely prudential obligations. However, as I have tried to demonstrate, the law at its basic level does not operate in the way the classic extended imperative model suggests. It does not state: do not kill, or else you will be killed. It does not operate by telling us what to do and then threatening us with the use of force in order to get us to do what we should have done without coercion. Rather, it permits the use of force in certain conditions by declaring it lawful. The obligation is secondary to this permission of the use of force. The extended imperative model or the similar Hartian requirement of '*voluntary* cooperation in a *coercive* system'[34] purports to give us two independent obligations: first there is the primary, free-standing obligation supposedly created by the legal demand and then there is the prudential 'obligation'

---

[34] Hart, *Concept of Law*, 198. Original emphasis.

created by the threat of sanction. The trouble with this model is that in one obligation it aims too high and in the other it aims too low: the free-standing obligation supposedly created by a mere legal demand can never be generated and the prudential obligation is too weak be called an obligation.

For the Pure Theory, conversely, there is only one legal obligation: the one based on the categorical permission to use force. It is neither a primary or free-standing obligation nor is it merely prudential. It is not primary because it is derived from a permission; it is not merely prudential because its validity is not dependent merely on my motives. The difference is that, whilst the purely prudential obligation is derived from a threat, the mixed obligation is derived from a categorical permission. The mixed obligation, whilst being hypothetical, is still not *purely* prudential, because its content is dependent on a categorical norm. The prudential obligation derived from a threat, however, has no categorical component.

Purely prudential norms are unattractive norms to base legal obligations on because they are unstable norms in the sense that bindingness depends on both the motive I have set myself and the credibility of the threat. If legal obligation were purely prudential, then I ought not to kill only because I want to stay alive and the threat is credible. If I did not care about my life or the treat were unreal, then the obligation not to kill would fall away. Take the following two statements:

(a)   If I do not want to be killed, I ought not to kill someone.
(b)   If I do not want the killing of me to be lawful, I ought not to kill someone.

Statement (a) is a hypothetical and merely prudential claim, whereas statement (b) is a mixed claim. It is hypothetical without being merely prudential. The difference between the two statements is the end that I have set myself: whilst in (a) the end is 'not being killed', in (b) the end is 'not rendering a killing of myself lawful'. Whilst (a) is justified by the credibility of a threat, (b) is justified by the validity of a norm. So, whilst (a) depends on two empirical facts, namely my motive and the credibility of the threat, (b) depends on only one empirical fact, namely, my motive. It does not depend on the credibility of a threat since the likelihood of me being killed is irrelevant for (b). What matters for (b) is that by killing someone I *ipso iure et facto* render a killing of me lawful. This follows necessarily as a matter of law. Even if no one threatened to kill me or no one were able to kill me, even if I believed that I killed the last person alive so that there was on one left to kill me, the result of my killing would still be that killing me would be lawful.

As a system of permissions, the law creates obligations by cutting through obligations, by absolving obligations, by returning to the naturalistic baseline. The law creates hypothetically valid obligations by cancelling categorically valid obligations. I might think that I am under a categorical obligation derived, say, from natural law to abstain from using force. I might be certain that I have a natural duty not to kill anyone. However, the law allows me to use force under certain conditions, to kill others under certain conditions, which puts other people under the hypothetical obligation to abstain from establishing those conditions. Human law 'condones what natural law condemns'[35] and thus creates a hypothetical permission by cancelling a seemingly categorical one. To characterise this relation and exchange of obligations as merely a prudential one would be to misunderstand the normative stakes at play. The question normally is: how can the law be justified to create obligations? The answer of the Pure Theory is: the law does not directly create obligations. The law only directly undermines obligations. The law is a social technique that uses moral scepticism and nihilism as the bedrock of its normative claim. It is in this sense that law and morality are not only unconnected but also, in a deep sense, opposed. It is in this sense that the law is a critique of morality as ideology.

At its heart, the Pure Theory thus works not from a relativistic but from a rather realistic understanding of morality. Of course, we all tend to believe that our own moral outlook is fully rational. However, what is more likely the case is that whatever moral theory and moral intuition we follow, it is only in part rational. Many of our moral convictions are very likely themselves pathological, they might flow from neurotic uptightness, projected feelings of guilt, confirmation bias, reaction formation, certain framings of issues learned in childhood and so on. The law, in a sense, remedies parts of these problems by setting us free from morality. The law allows things which I could not allow myself based only on my own moral reasoning. Or, put differently, we can allow ourselves more collectively than we can each allow ourselves individually. This is why for many the law stands high above morality. This is why for Hegel, for instance, the positive law, being a more concrete expression of objective spirit, represents a higher standpoint than subjective morality and why moral philosophy is part of the philosophy of right, but not vice versa.

To put it in very rough, emblematic terms: within jurisprudence, one has to choose between Rome and Athens.[36] Legal philosophers, being philosophers, tend to choose Athens. The Pure Theory has chosen Rome. Why Rome needs to be chosen over Athens has also been highlighted by Giambattista Vico.[37]

---

[35] Kant (n 17) 280 (XXVII, 516).

[36] Jerusalem, as the emblem of a political theology or a theological legality, is excluded for the modern world. How this defines the modern age and produces aporia of its own has been argued by Leo Strauss. See L Strauss, 'Jerusalem and Athens: Some Introductory Reflections' (1967) 43 *Commentary* 43.

[37] G Vico, *The New Science of Giambattista Vico*, trans TG Bergin and MH Fisch (Ithaca, Cornell University Press, 1948).

He argued that, following the example of Socrates, Greek philosophy, which was mainly metaphysical, has put itself more and more in opposition to the positive law and the positive custom of the *polis*. It has thus driven a wedge between philosophy and social practice, a separation which was in the end fatal for the entire Greek culture. Thus separated from social practice and from politics expressed in the positive law, philosophy became more and more a purely private matter, and as such took the necessary course via the indifference of stoicism to the despair of scepticism. This separation of philosophy and political system also had to undercut the latter in the end. In Rome, conversely, there was little philosophy isolated from public life. Rather, legal thought was grounded in wisdom and political life itself was philosophical. It is from this legal wisdom that the legal permissions emerge.

VI. EXCLUSIONARY PERMISSIONS?

Let us return from these lofty regions to the more mundane and sober. Does the Razian category of exclusionary permissions add anything to the analysis of permissions offered above? I do not think so. But let me expand: Raz correctly argues that the 'distinction between strong and weak permissions as it is commonly drawn makes little sense',[38] that both weak and strong permissions have the same normative force and express only a linguistic difference.[39] This is certainly true and, as stated in my argument, I partly rely on these Razian claims. After questioning this difference, however, Raz goes on to introduce a different category of permissions, which he calls exclusionary permissions. These permissions do not simply state that a certain act is permitted, but are designed as secondary reasons—namely, they are supposed to allow one to disregard certain reasons. Raz thinks that these reasons are necessary to explain supererogation, ie cases where the performance of an act is praiseworthy whilst at the same time the omission is not blameworthy. Supererogation is difficult to explain: the praiseworthiness of the performance indicates that, on the balance of reasons, there are reasons to act, whereas the non-blameworthiness of the omission indicates that, on the balance of reason, there are no such reasons. Raz's famous solution is that 'an act is a supererogatory act only

---

[38] Raz, *Practical Reason* (n 13) 88.

[39] 'Does anything turn on whether an obligation is imposed on people over thirty or on all with an exception for those under thirty? Are we to say that if the law is formulated in the first way then those under thirty have a weak permission to refrain from the action required of their elders, whereas if it is formulated in the second way they have a strong permission?': Raz, *Practical Reason* (n 13) 88.

if it is an act which one ought to do on the balance of reasons and yet one is permitted not to act on the balance of reasons'.[40]

Exclusionary permissions, if they made sense, would indeed explain supererogation. But do they make sense? Applying Raz's own broader framework of practical reason, it is hard to see that they do. Raz stresses that exclusionary permissions have to be strong permissions.[41] But he also argues that there is no normative difference between strong and weak permissions. To make matters worse, in the context of an analysis of exclusionary permissions, he goes so far as to claim that 'weak permissions contribute nothing to practical reason',[42] yet at the same time he argues that they can be granted: 'Both weak and exclusionary permissions can be granted. One grants a weak permission if one can and does change the reasons against an action so that its omission is no longer required.'[43] But if weak permissions do not contribute anything, why should they ever be granted? This makes little sense. Raz's example for a weak permission granted is the following: 'If a person owes money to another and his creditor waives his right to the debt he thereby gives his debtor a weak permission not to pay the debt.'[44] But this weak permission clearly does contribute to practical reasoning!

Secondly, the entire concept of exclusionary permission is more mysterious than it first appears: if an exclusionary permission is considered to be a 'permission to disregard a reason' and if, as Raz insists, this permission has to be considered to be a strong permission, then there must be an 'obligation to regard a reason' from which this permission alleviates one. Such an 'obligation to regard a reason' is necessary to make sense of exclusionary permissions. However, how should such an obligation be accommodated in Raz's system of practical reason? It is an essential part of Raz's project to explain obligations in terms of secondary reasons. But if we are in turn related to reasons via obligations or permissions, then we would have entered an infinite regress: if I have an obligation to regard a reason and if obligation means that I have an exclusionary reason, then the question arises whether or not I have an obligation to regard this exclusionary reason, which in turn can only be explained in terms of other exclusionary reasons and so on. It makes perfect sense to say that I have *reason* to disregard a reason, but it cannot make sense to argue that I have an *obligation* to regard or disregard a reason. Because of this, it cannot make sense to speak of a permission to disregard a reason. Thus, the entire

[40] ibid 94.
[41] ibid 90.
[42] ibid.
[43] ibid 96.
[44] ibid.

concept of exclusionary permission does not make sense. Practical reason is based on the idea that I either have a reason or I do not have a reason. Given this basic idea, it is hard to understand what an obligation to regard a reason amounts to.

So, when Raz comes to the conclusion that norms cannot grant weak permissions and that 'a weak permission has no normative force',[45] this not only flatly contradicts what he wrote before ('there is no difference in normative force' between weak and strong permissions[46]), but also shows that the account he offers is confused.

---

[45] ibid 97.
[46] ibid 88.

5

The Law as a Schema of Interpretation

I. INTRODUCTION

IN THE PREVIOUS chapters, I have argued that the law permits the use of force by declaring lawful the use of force. But what does it mean to 'declare lawful' the use of force? How does the law do that? How does it set down or change the meaning of acts?

According to the Pure Theory, the law does things by schematising inter-pretation, which is, in a sense, the most primitive operation of the law. In what follows, I will try to explain what a schema of interpretation is, how it differs from legal fictions and institutional facts, and how understanding the law as a schema of interpretation explains the law's specific mode of ordering society.

To get a sense of how the Pure Theory conceptualises the working of the law, we can take the following three examples:

(a)   In a room, a majority of the people stand up and say 'Aye' after a docu-ment has been circulated that contains the two sentences: 'Anyone who takes someone else's property is a thief. Thieves shall be executed.'
(b)   Peter takes Johns property.
(c)   Peter is executed.

In all three cases, the law operates as a schema of interpretation. In (a), the constitution schematises the interpretation of the goings-on as the enactment of a statute. In (b), the statute just enacted schematises the interpretation of Peter as being a thief. In (c), the statute just enacted schematises the killing of Peter as lawful. In the previous chapter, I have argued that all law operates by permitting the use of force. In this chapter, I will argue that the law permits the use of force by schematising interpretation—thus, all law fundamentally schematises interpretation.

'Interpretation' here is taken in the conventional meaning of understanding 'something as something'.[1] 'Schema' refers to the circumstance that the law

---

[1] KO Apel, *Understanding and Explanation. A Transcendental-Pragmatic Perspective*, trans G Warnke (Cambridge, MA, MIT Press, 1984); HG Gadamer, 'Text and Interpretation' in DF Michelfelder and RE Palmer (eds), *Dialogue and Deconstruction: The Gadamer–Derrida Encounter* (Albany, State

itself is not yet the interpretation. The positive law is the condition, the framework for a specific interpretation that intends to be a legal interpretation.

II. SCHEMATA, FICTIONS AND INSTITUTIONAL FACTS

What, then, is a schema? To start with, the law as a schema of interpretation must not be confused with a fiction. Peter, for instance, is not treated *as if* he were a thief. He *is* a thief—full stop. A fiction, conversely, is best understood as an assumption against firm knowledge.[2] However, here it is not the case that we assume that Peter is a thief even though we know that he is not a thief; it is also not the case that we assume that in (a) Parliament has enacted a statute even though we know that it has not; and, finally, it is not the case that in (c) we assume that killing Peter is lawful even though it is not. In functioning as a schema of interpretation, the law does not assume anything against firm knowledge.

Rather than being analogous to fictions, the law as a schema of interpretation is much closer to what has been called an institutional fact, ie to an understanding of legal rules as not regulative but fundamentally constitutive rules.[3] In what follows, I will briefly introduce this distinction between regulative and constitutional facts, and defend it against some criticism. After that, however, I will argue that, whilst illuminating some important aspects of the schema of interpretation, the latter cannot be fully explained as a rule constituting institutional facts.

As is well known, constitutive rules establish institutional facts by telling us that 'A counts as X in C': in a certain context C, a certain brute fact A counts as institutional fact X. In the context of a game of chess, moving a pawn to the last row of the field counts as promotion. The above examples all appear to be institutional facts: in (a) the standing up seems to count as 'enactment of a statute', in (b) the taking of property seems to count as 'theft' and in

---

University of New York Press, 1989) 30. See also H Lindahl, 'Dialectic and Revolution: Confronting Kelsen and Gadamer on Legal Interpretation' (2003) 24 *Cardozo Law Review* 769, who tries to show that in an encounter of Kelsen and Gadamer, the former is able to turn the tables on the project of a philosophical hermeneutics. Kelsen's doctrines of 'schema of interpretation' and of the basic norm can feature as a radicalisation of Gadamerian themes and should allow the Pure Theory to rejoin the 'hermeneutic turn' of modern philosophy. It is, for instance, only in presupposing the legal order, ie in presupposing the basic norm, that Gadamer can close his hermeneutic circle in the paradigmatic field of legal interpretation.

[2] It is defined as an *assumptio contra veritatem pro veritate in re certa*. See P Oliver, *Legal Fictions in Practice and Legal Science* (Rotterdam, Rotterdam University Press, 1975). See also M Del Mar et al (eds), *Legal Fictions in Theory and Practice* (Cham, Springer, 2015).

[3] See JR Searle, *The Construction of Social Reality* (London, Penguin 1995).

(c) the killing of Peter seems to count as 'lawful execution'. That, despite some overlap, this interpretation does not fully convey what is meant by a scheme of interpretation will be developed below in the next sub-section.

Here, I want to briefly engage the criticism that the distinction between regulative and constitutive rules does not make sense. I want to do that because the Pure Theory's notion of a scheme of interpretation relies, if not on exactly this distinction, then on a very similar one.

One classic line of criticism is that the distinction between constitutive and regulative rules is spurious, ie that all regulative rules are also constitutive and that all constitutive rules are also regulative. Jaap Hage has recently made an effort to argue that 'all rules are constitutive and that strictly speaking no rule guides behaviour', and that 'therefore Searle's opposition between regulative rules and constitutive ones is a bogus one'.[4] Joseph Raz has made the similar but more extensive claim that it follows from Searle's own account 'that all rules are both regulative and constitutive',[5] indicating that the distinction cannot be very useful. Since Raz's is a similar but broader claim than Hage's, I will engage with the former's.

Raz argues that whether we call a rule regulative or constitutive does not depend on the rule itself but only on the angle under which we approach it. For Searle, a rule is identified as a regulative rule if it regulates a behaviour that can be described along the same lines independently of whether the rule exists or not; conversely, a rule is identified as a constitutive rule if the behaviour in question has certain qualities which it would not have were it not for the rule.[6] However, Raz argues that, according to this definition, every seemingly constitutive rule can be described as regulative and vice versa. Take the case of someone saying 'I promise' and a constitutive rule that turns that act into an actual promise. According to Raz, we can describe the fact 'saying "I promise"' in such a way that it specifies an act which is 'in accordance with the rules in a way that could be given regardless of whether or not there is such a rule'.[7] This, Raz claims, makes the rule regulative. At the same time, however, the description 'promising' describes an action 'in accordance with the rules in a way which could not be given if there were no such rules'.[8] This, in turn, makes the rule constitutive.

---

[4] J Hage, 'Separating Rules from Normativity' in M Araszkiewicz et al (eds), *Problems of Normativity, Rules and Rule-Following* (Cham, Springer, 2015) 13–30. See also J Hage, 'The Deontic Furniture of the World' in J Stelmach et al (eds), *The Many Faces of Normativity* (Kraków, Copernicus Center, 2013) 73–114.

[5] J Raz, *Practical Reason and Norms* (Oxford, Oxford University Press, 1999) 109.

[6] J Searle, *Speech Acts. An Essay in the Philosophy of Language* (Cambridge, Cambridge University Press, 1969) 35.

[7] Raz (n 5) 109.

[8] ibid.

I am not sure that this is a convincing rebuttal of Searle's position. Fernando Atria has even called Raz's argument 'a clear non sequitur'.[9] First of all, even if it were the case that for the examples Raz has presented one could find both a regulative and a constitutive description, it does not follow from that alone that this is true for all rules. Whilst for the act-description 'saying "I promise"' we can indeed find the rule-dependent description 'promising', the same is not the case for the act-description of 'giving to the poor'. If there is a rule demanding that we give to the poor, then the act of giving to the poor does not yield an act-description that depends on the rule and that goes beyond the mere triviality of 'rule-conforming act'.[10]

Secondly, apart from failing to demonstrate that all rules are constitutive, I am not sure Raz has succeeded in demonstrating that all rules are regulative in Searle's sense either: let us start with a rule of the constitutive form 'A counts as X in C', namely, 'Saying "I promise" counts as promising'. Raz seems to suggest that we can take this rule to be a regulative rule since we can describe 'Saying "I promise"' independently of the rule. However, the ability to describe the A-term of a constitutive rule independently of the rule cannot be a criterion for something to be a regulative rule! We can, of course, describe the A-term independently of the rule, otherwise we could not apply the rule in the first place. The A-term is the brute-fact input into the rule and the X-term is the institutional-fact output of the rule. The input exists independently of the rule, the output does not. Take grunting. I can grunt and this can be described independently of any rule, say by the act-description 'uttering the sound "oomph"'. Now, if we had the rule 'Uttering the sound "oomph" counts as submission in the game of Potlatch', then this would provide a new act-description which a regulative rule does not provide. From the fact that we can still describe 'uttering the sound "oomph"' independently of the new rule, it simply does not follow that this rule is regulative. This is so since the criterion for something to be a constitutive rule is that the X-term is non-trivially different from the A-term.

A somewhat similar criticism has been levelled against the Searlean distinction by Neil MacCormick. He also claims that 'the boundary between regulative and constitutive is unclear in Searle's schema'.[11] I have, I hope,

---

[9] F Atria, 'Games and the Law: Two Models of Institution' (1999) 85 *Archiv für Rechts- und Sozialphilosophie* 309, 315. For a criticism of Raz basing the difference of constitutive and regulative rules on so-called 'status rules', see F Hindriks, 'Constitutive Rules, Language, and Ontology' (2009) 71 *Erkenntnis* 253.

[10] This is exactly the route via which Hage tries to secure the constitutive nature of all regulative rules, ie they constitute deontic facts. It is also precisely the 'trivial sense' of constitutive nature of all rules which Searle conceded. See Searle (n 6) 35; Hage, 'Separating Rules' (n 6).

[11] N MacCormick, 'Norms, Institutions, and Institutional Facts' (1998) 17 *Law and Philosophy* 301, 335.

dealt with this argument above in my discussion of Raz's criticism. But MacCormick adds two further criticisms of Searle's account. First, he argues that it is unclear how a Searlean constitutive rule is a rule in the normative sense. By a rule in the normative sense, he is referring to a rule that is 'a guide to judgement and conduct'.[12] It should not be too difficult to see how a constitutive rule is a guide to judgement: the normativity of the rule lies precisely in the fact that it purports to determine judgement. Without the rule 'Uttering the sound "oomph" counts as submission in the game of Potlatch', I cannot come to a conclusion about what grunting in this context means. With the rule, I can reach a final judgement about the issue. But if this rule does not immediately tell us what to do, why should its guidance of judgement be called 'normative'? It is certainly normative in the wider sense of being non-factual. Apart from the stipulation in the rule, there is no factual link between 'uttering the sound of "oomph"' and 'submission'. The rule does not intend to represent a reality, it makes it. It has, as Searle and others have put it, a double direction of fit $\updownarrow$ in that it 'creates the very reality it represents'.[13] So whilst, in the first analysis, not being 'normative' in the narrow sense of possessing a world-to-mind direction of fit $\uparrow$, constitutive rules are normative in possessing more than a mind-to-world direction of fit $\downarrow$. I added the qualification 'in the first analysis' since, in second analysis, as we have seen, a constitutive rule may very well possess normativity in the narrow sense of a world-to-mind direction of fit $\uparrow$: if grunting counts as submission, one might be indirectly directed to avoid grunting. So constitutive rules can guide both judgement and conduct.

MacCormick's second worry is that

> Searle's canonical 'x counts as y in circumstances c' seems unhelpfully over-broad, for almost anything can count as almost anything else in apt circumstances. A bottle can count as a weapon in a pub brawl without any of these concepts having to be considered as a social institution, or a legal institution, or a cultural one either. On the other hand, it is true that a glass vessel with a narrow neck used for storing liquids counts as a bottle. This may indeed tell me something about the noun 'bottle' or even the concept 'bottle' within the English language. If there is anything we should call an institutional element here, this would relate to the sense in which nouns or concepts might be characterized as institutions within languages; but this would not give helpful information about institutions in the wider practical sense with which the institutional theory of law is concerned.[14]

---

[12] ibid 335.

[13] J Searle, *Making the Social World. The Structure of Human Civilization* (Oxford, Oxford University Press, 2010), 16.

[14] N MacCormick, *Institutions of Law. An Essay in Legal Theory* (Oxford, Oxford University Press, 2007) 37; MacCormick (n 11) 335.

MacCormick is, of course, entirely correct that a bottle can be used as a weapon in a pub brawl and thus can also 'count as' one. This, however, only establishes that there can be many informal institutional facts and that we might indeed want to call language an institution—maybe the ultimate institution. The argument does not, however, establish that the concepts involved cannot be considered 'as a social institution, or a legal institution, or a cultural one either'.[15] That the law can, and very often actually does, transform, mould or contradict these informal, implicit rules by issuing formal explicit rules, eg by stipulating that carrying a bottle upside down at its neck counts (or does not count) as carrying a weapon, rather shows that what we are dealing with here are actually social institutions. As I will argue below, it is precisely those informal contents of meaning that the law affects and alters in order to do what it does. If those ordinary meanings were of a different kind than the legal meaning, it would be hard to see how the law could relate to, let alone alter, them.

I thus think that the Searlean distinction is prima facie plausible.

III. SCHEMATA AND IMAGINATION

That the Searlean distinction is in principle sound and illuminating does, however, not perforce mean that the law is best understood in its terms. In what follows, I will argue that it needs a certain tweaking or addition to capture the full range of meaning that is conveyed by the idea of a schema of interpretation.

The problem with the Searlean theory applied to the law is the following: according to Searle's model in establishing an institutional fact, the constitutive rule creates a second reality, different from the first reality of brute facts. This second reality has its existence and actuality in 'collective recognition or acceptance'.[16] The schema of interpretation, conversely, does not intend to create a second, fictional or institutional, world. To return to our example above, the law does not tell us that Peter *counts as* a thief. Rather Peter *is* a thief—full stop. The schema does not create a game and take scores. Rather than establishing a fictional or institutional account, rather than creating a second world, the rules schematise our interpretation of the first world itself. They are aimed at the first world itself. The law, therein, has both a constitutive and a cognitive function.

---

[15] N MacCormick, *Institutions of Law. An Essay in Legal Theory* (Oxford, Oxford University Press, 2007) 37; MacCormick (n 11) 335.
[16] Searle (n 13) 8.

By 'cognitive function', I want to refer to the fact that in the schematising interpretation, the law also wants to tell us something about the world that exists independently of that schematisation. To make sense of this claim, it is helpful to have a brief look at Kantian philosophy. Here, the notion of a 'schema' links to the faculty of imagination, the faculty of making present something which is not actually present in sensual perception. For Kant, imagination is not just the faculty that allows us to daydream and invent things, to write novels and paint paintings; rather, it is a crucial constitutive element in forming objective knowledge of the world, which allows us to understand objectivity as objective. Without imagination, Kant argues, we would not be able to get access to the objective world as objective. The schema is what links our conceptual activity to the world. It is not to be confused with a mere image; rather, it is what links the concept with the world:

> No image of a triangle would ever be adequate to the concept of it. For it would not attain the generality of the concept, which makes this valid for all triangles, right or acute, etc., but would always be limited to one part of this sphere. The schema of the triangle can never exist anywhere except in thought, and signifies a *rule of the synthesis of the imagination* with regard to pure shapes in space.[17]

For Kant, the schema is thus 'a rule of the synthesis of the imagination'. That means it is not a static determined image, but an image of images, a procedure that allows us to construct images.

> The concept of a dog signifies a rule in accordance with which my imagination can specify the shape of a four-footed animal in general, without being restricted to any single particular shape that experience offers me or any possible image that I can exhibit in concreto. This schematism of our understanding with regard to appearances and their mere form is a hidden art in the depths of the human soul, whose true operations we can divine from nature and lay unveiled before our eyes only with difficulty.[18]

The larger idea behind this is that, since the objectivity of the world as such cannot directly be perceived, imagination has to project it as an order onto the world—an order, however, which is not merely superimposed on the real world, but which makes up the very reality of the real. Imagination, for instance, allows us to not only think of objects as non-perspectival entities, but to actually experience them as such, even though by definition we can never

---

[17] I Kant, *Critique of Pure Reason*, trans P Guyer (Cambridge, Cambridge University Press, 1998) 273, A 141/B 180. It was Hannah Arendt who first saw the general relevance of the notion of imagination and the schema. See H Arendt, *The Life of the Mind* (San Diego, Harvest, 1978) 100–101.

[18] Kant (n 17) B 180–81.

perceive them non-perspectively since all we ever see from a given object are different perspectives.[19] Imagination adds in schematic form not to thought, but to experience, those qualities which we do not and cannot perceive, including objectivity as such.

Wilfried Sellars, for instance, put it as follows:

> Kant claims that the very same rule-governed conceptual activity that occurs in the free-play of the imagination constitutes perceptual experience, when it is guided by independent reality. According to this interpretation, the 'productive imagination' (which is Kant's term for the faculty that generates intuitive representings of the form 'this cube') provides the subject-terms of perceptual judgments.[20]

In a similar way, the law operating as a scheme of interpretation is 'a rule of the synthesis' not of individual imagination, but of collective imagination. Therein the law does not imagine a second world, where it takes scores, but tells us something along the following lines: you might not have noticed, you might not have realised it, but by taking someone else's property Peter is actually already a thief. It might not be readily visible, but this is what has actually happened in the world. The rules thus do not talk about fictions, they do not establish separate institutional facts; rather, they allow us to experience a certain reality in its totality.[21] In allowing us to do this, they also allow us to bring order to the world. In the next chapter, I will discuss how exactly the law functioning as a schema of interpretation brings order to the world.

[19] 'Consider as an example a perceptual experience such as that you might enjoy if you were to hold a bottle in your hand with eyes closed. You have a sense of the presence of the whole bottle, even though you only make contact with the bottle at a few isolated points ... One way we might try to explain this is by observing that you draw on your knowledge of what bottles are ... You bring to bear your conceptual skills. This is doubtless right. But it does not, I think, do justice to the phenomenology of the experience. For, crucially, your sense of the presence of the bottle is a sense of its perceptual presence. That is, you do not merely think or infer that there is a bottle present, in the way, say, that you think or infer that there is a room next door. The presence of the bottle is not inferred or surmised. It is experienced.' A Noë, 'Is the World a Grand Illusion?' in A Noë (ed), *Is the Visual World a Grand Illusion?* (Thorverton, Imprint Academic, 2002) 8–9.

[20] W Sellars, *Kant's Transcendental Metaphysics: Sellar's Cassirer Lectures Notes and Other Essays* (Atascadero, Ridgeview, 2002) 273. See also G Banham, *Kant's Transcendental Imagination* (London, Palgrave Macmillan 2005). Henry Allison thinks that whilst these Sellerian interpretations 'make contact with deep Kantian themes, they are somewhat problematic as interpretations of Kant'. See H Allison, *Kant's Transcendental Idealism. An Interpretation and Defence* (New Haven, Yale University Press, 2004), 187.

[21] 'It may be remembered, from Kelsen, that norms serve as a schema of interpretation. They invest events and structures with significance ... Norms can be used, therefore, to idealise realities and thus to render social facts expressive of ideals or of something evil.' A Somek, 'Idealisation, De-politicization and Economic Due Process: System Transition in the European Union' in B Iancu (ed), *The Law/Politics Distinction in Contemporary Public Law Adjudication* (Utrecht, Eleven International, 2009).

IV. LAW AND ORDER

There are two ways of bringing order to the world: by acting or by thinking.

We can either come up with a pattern, principle or plan that we can apply to an unordered chaotic state of affairs by acting in the world according to the plan (eg we pick up the laundry from the floor and put it where it belongs) or we can leave the state of affairs as it is and try to find a principle or rule that describes the state of affairs in such a way that what originally seemed chaotic actually turns out to be ordered.

Take the following example: I ask my daughter to tidy up her room. Because she is a good child, she does what I tell her and puts all the laundry that is lying around the floor in the laundry box. Now imagine I also tell my son to tidy up his room. However, rather than doing what I tell him, my son stares at the laundry and after a while he tells me that there is already an intricate order, which I failed to see: the laundry on the floor actually traces the outline of the Rhine border and he is re-enacting the Franco-Prussian war.

That we can bring order to the world by thinking about the world might seem strange at first. However, it is not confined to children's rooms and games. The sciences, for instance, bring order to the world by thinking about it. They do not make order in the world by interfering with it and actively ordering it, but rather they find order. After centuries of scientific treatment, what used to be a tempest of capricious weather phenomena is now a series of more or less predictable events. What used to be considered the arbitrary whims of gods or pure chance are now an at least partially calculable order. Science is the process of finding an ever more intricate order in the world.

The first way *imprints* patterns onto the world, the second *finds* patterns in the world. The first approach is the way in which morality orders the world; the second is the way in which science orders it. Both have a different direction of fit.

Morality tells us how things ought to be. It sets up a template of how affairs or actions ought to be, compares affairs and actions to this template, and demands that the world be brought into correspondence with the template. It *imprints* patterns.

The peculiarity that order can be brought about both by acting and by thinking is owing to the puzzling nature of the concept 'order', which is concurrently something present in the world and something only in our heads, something actual and intellectual, and both objective and subjective.[22]

One might be tempted to think that science does not actually bring order to the world, or that it does so only in a figurative sense. After all, the order has to

---

[22] For a very accessible account of how science treats order, see M Gell-Mann, *The Quark and the Jaguar: Adventures in the Simple and the Complex* (New York, Henry Holt, 1994) 28.

already have been 'out there' in the first place to be found in a putative second step. From a theoretical point of view, this might indeed pose very complicated metaphysical questions, which might be of prime philosophical interest. From a practical point of view, however, there is little difference between the two forms of ordering: an objective, albeit invisible, order is practically just as irrelevant as no order at all. From the practical point of view, both ways of ordering have the same effect: first there was no order, then there was order.

For us, the important question is: according to which of the two paradigms does the positive law bring order to states of affairs? Is it more like morality or more like science?

As I have repeatedly argued, within jurisprudence the positive law is thought about predominantly under the moralist paradigm. Legal norms are seen as demands, standards or mandates, and are accordingly treated as being structurally similar to moral norms. It thus seems only natural to think that the law, too, is attempting to change the world by setting up a template and demanding that the world be less like it actually is and more like the template. Note that most positivists also adopt this moralist model.

The Pure Theory does not claim that the law is like science. However, the law's way of bringing order to the world sits somewhere between making order and finding it: it brings order to the world by *superimposing* or *projecting* order. The law brings order to states of affairs not by telling the world how it ought to be, but by describing the world as it is already ordered: as we have seen, at the base level, the law does not attempt to create order by demanding that Peter does not steal but, rather, establishes an order by declaring Peter to be a thief, or, more accurately, by schematising the interpretation of Peter as a thief. As such, it goes far beyond mere Searlean constitutive rules which create institutional facts out of nothing.

To illustrate the proposed understanding of the relation between law and order, take a queue. When people stand in a line one behind the other, this is quite clearly an ordered state of affairs. Is such a queue not created by demanding that whoever joins the queue ought to do so at the end? So is order not brought into the world by demanding orderly action? Well, I do not think this is the correct way of understanding a queue in particular, or social order in general: imagine a doctor's waiting room, where some people sit and others stand, without any clear order, particularly not the order of people forming an orderly line. However, the fact that we do not specifically notice any order does not mean that there is none: clearly, people are actually ordered in terms of their height, their age, their weight, the number of hairs on their heads, how many siblings they have, or in relation to the time they entered the room. There is, actually, an infinite number of orders that can be found in this room. Now, any of those objective orders can be picked out to form an informal queue. It might be the age, the time people entered the room or the number on the ticket each of them carries in their pocket. So we might find out that whereas we believed that the people in the room were an unordered mess, they might actually form an informal queue where, say, it is always the turn of the oldest person in the room. Alternatively, the rule applied could be that it is the turn of the person who arrived first or of the person who has the ticket with the lowest number on it. Whatever the rule applied, it creates order in the room without changing anything in the room or demanding any action. Rather, the rule picks out an existing order. It turns a mere mass of people (chaos) into a queue (order) without physically interfering with it or demanding anything. As soon as one of these qualities is picked out, people will, of course, change their behaviour in relation to the picked-out quality: they will come earlier, send the tallest or oldest member of the family, pick up a number from the ticket dispenser as soon as they come in, etc. This adaptive behaviour then takes on the guise of a 'demand'. But the demand is not what is primary; it is the picking out of a certain order that 'creates' the order.

We can now see that the actual line of one person standing behind another is but a special case of this more general understanding of how rules create order not by demanding some action, but by picking out an ordering quality. In the case of a line, the quality picked out to determine whose turn it next is 'who arrived first'. The line is more of an aide-memoire to this first-come-first-serve principle.[23] Different aides are conceivable, like numbers on tickets. A line thus does not start with a demand but with an agreement on which of the various orders actually out there in the world are picked out as relevant to determining whose turn it is. A queue, after all, does not determine whose turn it ought to be, but whose turn it is. The demand 'Please stand at the back of the line!' is not a primary one, but a derivative demand flowing from this settlement.

This is also how the law operates. It picks out an order in the world and thus creates order without needing to demand any action. The demands, rather, flow from behaviour adapting itself to this order. Thus, first comes the order, then the demand.

Now, aligning the law to the moralistic paradigm makes a distinction of law from morality necessary, and it is hardly a surprise that a jurisprudence wedded to this paradigm will spend most of its intellectual effort on keeping law distinct from morality. Conversely, the closer alignment to the cognitive paradigm will make a distinction between law and the sciences, and especially

---

[23] That a queue cannot fully be understood as an aide-memoire but that things are more complex is indicated by the fact that one might give up one's spot in the queue for someone else who has only just arrived. The person taking the spot will then be served before people at the back of the line who actually came before him. So the quality picked out is a mix between 'who came first' and the more formal quality of 'who stands in front of the line'.

sociology, necessary. The anticipation and delivery of such a differentiation by the historic Pure Theory is a feature that is often overlooked. The Pure Theory appreciates that as a schema of interpretation, the law stands in competition not so much with morality as with sociology: after all, a sociologist is also in the business of trying to tell us what a state is, what theft is, what a statute is, what poverty is, etc. I think the often-used epithet 'double purity', which also includes a purity from sociological admixtures, makes little sense and remains utterly incomprehensible when one does not take into account the shift towards a more cognitive paradigm and the ensuing tension with sociology that the Pure Theory effects.

As concerns this relation, the Pure Theory claims that the normativity of the law's schematisation of interpretation trumps the schemata of sociology and ordinary language: according to sociology, a people taking other peoples' property might be explained via analysis of classes and social stratification, but according to the law it is simply theft. So, in the end, the law is not purely cognitive, it does not attempt to accurately represent the world; rather, in its schematisations, in its projections of order to the world, it is not limited by a given order but can do so freely. The law thus operates as a collective schematisation of social reality.

It is the law itself and not legal science (ie a rationally organised systematic engagement with the positive law) which stands in competition with sociology. The Pure Theory's point is that the law itself has something resembling a sociology—just as it has a morality. It is only because the law itself is both sociological and moral in nature that the study of the law has to steer clear from moral and sociological considerations. If it did not, it would replace its object's sociology and morality with its own and it would thus miss its object. The purity of the Pure Theory is thus an epistemological demand.

Via its schemata of interpretation, the law thus, in a thoroughly Kantian sense, imagines a certain order by projecting it onto the social world. The law thus does not tell us what to do, but rather what we have done. It does not tell Peter not to steal, but it tells him and everybody else that by stealing he already is a thief and as a thief (in the above scheme) he can be killed with impunity. The crucial difference is the kind of imagination the law uses. The law thus does not change the world by imagining a more ideal state and then telling the world to be more like this imagination. Rather, it imagines an order as already actual within the world. We are always already queuing—we just do not know it yet.

6

Normative Monism

I. INTRODUCTION

AS WE HAVE seen, the Pure Theory claims that the law regulates society by schematising the interpretation of force or violence to the effect that, under certain conditions, the use of force is permitted. However, it is not only the law that claims to have something to say about the use of force or violence: morality, too, makes claims about the use of force, and its claims are likely to be much more prohibitive than the law's. What, then, is the exact relation between the law's permission of the use of force and morality's prohibition of the use of force?[1]

The Pure Theory is very often understood to simply argue that the law is conceptually independent from morality. But what is this supposed to mean? If the law claimed that X is permitted and morality claimed that it is not permitted, how much insight have we gained by finding out that the law's content is not determined by morality? It seems we have answered no question at all by claiming that the law allows X independently from the moral prohibition of X as long we have nothing to say about how the law's permission relates to the prohibition issued by morality. What we thus need is a theory that answers not only the question 'Is the content of the law dependent on any moral considerations?', but also 'What is the relation between the legal and moral claims?'

The Pure Theory is such a theory. According to this theory, law and morality do not and cannot stand in any relation to each other whatsoever, as they cannot both be considered to be valid at the same time. In what follows, I will defend this claim and argue that the validity of the law excludes the validity of morality and vice versa.[2]

This seemingly strange position follows from normative monism and constitutes what could be called normative jinx. It explains two things at the same

---

[1] I have made similar claims in C Kletzer, 'The Normative Jinx' [2017] *OJLS* gqx010. doi: 10.1093/ojls/gqx010.

[2] Kelsen himself changed his view on this issue significantly throughout his intellectual life, so it seems futile to try to pin the claims I am making on Kelsen. For Kelsen's version of a similar claim, see H Kelsen, *General Theory of Law and State* (Cambridge, MA, Harvard University Press, 1949) 407–18; H Kelsen, *Die philosophischen Grundlagen der Naturrechtslehre und des Rechtspositivismus* (Berlin, Heise, 1928).

time: what the true, paradoxical relation of law and morality is and why we find it so hard to understand.

This troubled relation is the consequence of the combination of two rather straightforward theses: normative monism and legal/moral incompatibilism. The first is simply the denial of normative pluralism. It claims that normative pluralism cannot appropriately account for the phenomenon of normativity and that if law and morality are to be considered valid simultaneously they have to be considered as parts of one normative system. The second is the claim that law and morality cannot be part of one normative system. What follows is that law and morality cannot be considered to be valid simultaneously.

In this chapter, I will present and defend both theses. I think that neither is particularly controversial; it is their combination that is problematic.

Whilst variants of legal/moral incompatibilism may be familiar from debates of philosophical anarchism and hard positivism, normative monism, in the way I present it here, faces the challenge of either sounding terribly implausible or, if made to sound less implausible, appearing to be trivial.

A normative monist denies the coherence of normative pluralism. A normative pluralist is someone who thinks that it is possible that there exist two or more normative systems which are valid independently of each other. For the normative pluralist, it must thus be possible that there exist two norms which, despite both being valid, still stand in no normative relation to each other. The normative monist denies this possibility. The structure of this debate is similar to the structure of the debate between the legal monist and the legal pluralist: whereas the legal pluralist (often a dualist) claims that it is conceivable that two norms, despite being legal norms, stand in no legal relation to each other, the legal monist denies this possibility.

The crux here is quite obviously what 'standing in a normative relation' means. I will try to answer this question. In order to do that, I will first look at the legal monism/pluralism debate to highlight what 'standing in a *legal* relation' means.

II. LEGAL MONISM

The legal pluralist argues that it is possible for two norms to be valid yet to stand in no legal relation to each other. A legal monist denies that this could ever be possible.[3] A legal monist argues that in every seemingly pluralistic

---

[3] In this chapter, I do not follow Hart's and Raz's view that a monist is someone who claims that in order to have a unified legal system it is sufficient that one legal system 'purports to validate' another. I know of no monist who would claim that. Certainly Kelsen, who is Hart's main target, would never have claimed such a thing. Quite clearly, Hart has set himself up a straw man here. See HLA Hart, *Essays in Jurisprudence and Philosophy* (Oxford, Clarendon Press,

set-up, a legal norm can be found that connects the two seemingly unrelated norms and unifies them within one legal system.[4] There is a weak and a strong version of legal monism. The weak version presents the *empirical* claim that for any two seemingly unrelated contemporary legal norms another legal norm will be found that connects these two norms and combines them into one normative system.[5] The strong claim, conversely, present the *logical* claim that, by necessity, for any two seemingly unrelated legal norms another legal norm has to exist that connects the two norms and combines them into one normative system. In this chapter, I will here defend the strong claim.[6]

On first reflection, legal monism of whatever stripe seems straightforwardly false. Many examples spring to mind that appear plainly to contradict legal monism. The criminal law of the Icelandic Althing, the WTO rules regulating technical barriers to trade and the customary Korean rules regulating clan membership must surely be elements of different legal systems? Just as tellingly, Lars Vinx points out that it would 'make no sense for a legal historian to argue that the legal system of the Roman Empire and of the Chinese Empire formed parts of one global legal system'.[7]

It thus looks as though legal monism is a non-starter. However, taking Vinx's example as the acid test for legal monism, let us imagine an Imperial Chinese norm (C) and an Imperial Roman norm (R). In order to make the test harder, let us assume, *contra veritatem*, that there were no economic or social relations between the Roman and Chinese peoples, and let us further assume that the

---

1983) 309; J Raz, *The Concept of Legal System. An Introduction to the Theory of Legal System* (Oxford, Oxford University Press, 1970) 95–109. For a critical discussion setting the debate straight, see L Vinx, 'Austin, Kelsen, and the Model of Sovereignty: Notes on the History of Modern Legal Positivism' in M Freeman and P Mindus (eds), *The Legacy of John Austin's Jurisprudence* (Cham, Springer, 2012) 51–71; L Vinx, 'The Kelsen–Hart Debate: Hart's Critique of Kelsen's Legal Monism Reconsidered' in DAJ Telman (ed), *Hans Kelsen in America: Selective Affinities and the Mysteries of Academic Influence* (Cham, Springer, 2016) 59–83.

[4] For Kelsen's version of international legal monism, see H Kelsen, *Das Problem der Souveränität und die Theorie dies Völkerrechts-Beitrag zu einer reinen Rechtslehre* (Vienna, JC Mohr, 1920); H Kelsen, *Reine Rechtslehre: Einleitung in die rechtswissenschaftliche Problematik* (Vienna, Deuticke, 1934). For a magisterial treatment of Kelsen's position on international law, see J von Bernstorff, *The Public International Law Theory of Hans Kelsen: Believing in Universal Law* (Cambridge, Cambridge University Press, 2010). For a classic discussion of legal monism in international law, see JG Starke, 'Monism and Dualism in the Theory of International Law' (1936) 17 *British Year Book of International Law* 74. For contemporary treatments, see J Crawford, *Chance, Order, Change: The Course of International Law, General Course on Public International Law* (Leiden, Brill 2014) 212–43; BI Bonafé, 'International Law in Domestic and Supranational Settings' in J Kammerhofer et al (eds), *International Legal Positivism in a Post-Modern World* (Cambridge, Cambridge University Press, 2014) 378.

[5] This is the claim presented by Lars Vinx. Vinx, 'The Kelsen-Hart Debate' (n 3).

[6] Lars Vinx thinks that Raz and Hart have managed to establish the falsity of the strong claim. Vinx, 'Austin, Kelsen' (n 3).

[7] Vinx, 'The Kelsen–Hart Debate' (n 3) 69.

Romans did not know about the Chinese and vice versa, and that there was accordingly not even rudimentary international law regulating the legal relation between the Romans and the Chinese. Let us finally assume that they could just as well have inhabited different planets in different galaxies.

Have we not here constructed a waterproof counter-example to the strong claim that any two valid norms must be part of one and the same legal system? The appearance is deceptive: if one were to take the point of view of Roman Imperial law, then, given our assumptions, there would be no valid Chinese law. Alternatively, if one were to take the point of view of Chinese Imperial law, there would be no valid Roman law. So, rather than establishing pluralism, in both cases one would end up with one legal system only and legal pluralism would thus not even be on the table as an option. In trying to defend pluralism, one has to take a position that allows R and C to be valid simultaneously. Such a point of view, which allows us to take R and C as both being valid legally, is a point of view that presupposes legal monism. Thus, pluralism arises as an option only when one has already assumed monism.

But does not the historian's point of view, looking back at two clearly separate normative systems, make sense? It does, but it does not really present a pluralist perspective in the required sense, since the historian's point of view is what Hart called a fully *external* one. Such an external point of view does not treat the norms in question as valid norms. They are only treated as 'valid' in a derivative sense of being part of a legal system and not as having any normative force.[8] Norms that are not valid do not exist as norms. The pluralism we have reached here is not a real pluralism. We defined pluralism as the independence of valid legal norms. All that the historian's pluralism can demonstrate is the plurality of unreal, imagined or historical norms. It is, of course, the case that there is a plurality of invalid norms, ie norms that no longer or not yet exist as norms. But this 'plurality' of non-existent things—if such talk makes any sense at all—can in no way refute legal monism.

This difference between valid (and thus existent) and non-valid (and thus non-existent) norms can be neatly illustrated by reference to just the Roman law that we have been talking about: until the late nineteenth century, Roman law was not only a subject of historic interest to German scholars, but was valid law to be applied by German courts.[9] The specific quality of a legal

---

[8] I will discuss further reasons for why I think we have to avoid separating validity from bindingness later in this chapter and also in the next chapter.

[9] For a discussion of Roman law, see C Kletzer, 'Custom and Positivity: An Examination of the Philosophical Ground of the Hegel–Savigny Controversy' in A Perreau-Saussine and J Murphy (eds), *The Nature of Customary Law: Philosophical, Historical and Legal Perspectives* (Cambridge, Cambridge University Press, 2007) 128. Savigny's opus magnum was aptly called *Das System des heutigen Römischen Rechts* ('The System of Today's Roman Law'). He wrote: 'Accordingly the exposition of today's Roman law, at which the present work is aimed, will need only

historian like Savigny looking at Roman law in 1840 was that he believed that in his historic scholarship he was uncovering valid law in the full sense of the term, ie law to be applied by courts. A contemporary legal historian can, of course, distinguish between Roman law that has been 'valid' and that which has not been 'valid'. This notion of 'validity', however, is a derivative one, dependent on the full notion of validity.

All of this will not suffice to convince the pluralist. After all, in our example, it appears plain and certain that R and C, whilst both legally valid, stand in no legal relation to each other. Both legal systems are strictly separated geographically and whilst R applies in the Roman Empire (and not in the Chinese Empire), C applies in the Chinese Empire (and not in the Roman Empire). So, given the strict separation of spheres of applicability, where should we find the legal relation which the monist claims is unavoidable if we want to assume two simultaneously valid legal norms?

Let us look more closely at this separation of applicability. What does it mean to claim that the spheres of applicability are separated? It means that, legally, the applicability of certain norms is limited to certain regions. A legal limitation of the applicability of norms can, however, only be effected by a legal norm that is superior to the norms the applicability of which is limited, ie a universal norm. Let us call such a norm 'U'. Now, this norm, which is superior to the norms with limited applicability, links the two geographically separated legal systems and unifies them into one legal system. So it is precisely this division of spheres of applicability that gives us the legal relation that monism claims is necessarily present.

There are at least three arguments to challenge the claim that this 'conferral of spheres of applicability' by norm U constitutes a legal relation uniting the two legal systems: first, one can argue that the relation of divided applicability is *not a legal relation* but is simply the fact of geographic separation; secondly, one can argue that even if one accepted that the conferral of spheres of validity were a legal fact, this fact does *not establish the unity* of the two systems; thirdly, one could argue that even if one accepted that a unity between the legal systems were established, this would be a unity in name only and would be *theoretically uninteresting*.

Let us consider the first argument first. Granted, the spatial separation of the two empires is certainly first and foremost a geographic fact. However, this fact alone does not bear legal significance. After all, the Roman provinces

---

few additions to become an exposition of the common law of Germany.' FC von Savigny, *System des heutigen Römischen Rechts* (Berlin, Veit, 1840) vol 1, 5. Savigny's system clearly laid claim to presenting valid law and thus a law that was directly applicable by the German courts. See R Scheuermann, *Einflüsse der historischen Rechtsschule auf die oberstrichterliche gemeinrechtliche Zivilrechtspraxis bis zum Jahre 1861* (Berlin, DeGruyter, 1972).

of *Germania Inferior* and *Arabia Petraea* were also spatially (and culturally) separated—and this separation does not have the legal significance that the separation between the two empires is claimed to have. So there must be some other criterion that distinguishes between the two cases and determines that, whilst in one case Roman law applies to both spatially separated regions, in the other case Roman law does not apply to both regions but only to one. Now, since any criterion that determines the conditions of the applicability of law is a *legal* criterion, the separation of the two systems is fundamentally a legal separation.

It thus turns out that, whilst at first it is legal monism that might seem counter-intuitive, it is ultimately legal pluralism that is paradoxical and rests on a misunderstanding: it fails to see that normative separation has to be a normative relation. Legal pluralism starts from the logically incoherent idea of two legal systems that are both normatively separated yet unrelated. For that to be possible, the highest norm of the one legal system must not apply to the other legal system. However, the fact that a norm does *not* apply somewhere is not a brute fact but a legal fact. Thus, there has to be an even higher norm that stipulates that the seemingly highest norm applying to the one legal system does not apply to the other legal system. This higher norm, by definition, applies to both legal systems and establishes legal monism. So, as soon as we think we have established pluralism (our highest norm does not apply there), what we have actually established is monism (there is a higher norm applying to both systems).

Let us now turn to the second argument. This argument accepts the refutation of the first and thus accepts that the conferral of spheres of applicability of the law is not simply a brute fact but also a legal fact. What it resists is the further conclusion that this legal fact by itself implies a legal relation between the two legal systems. After all, the limited spatial applicability of Roman law to the Roman Empire could be the legal result of a Roman Imperial rule R* and the limited spatial applicability of Chinese law to the Chinese Empire could be the legal result of a Chinese Imperial rule C*. The limitation of applicability could thus be seen to be effected entirely from within each legal system. Furthermore, the argument would run, R* and C* do not have to stand in any legal relation to each other whatsoever.

Or do they? Let us see if this argument can really deliver a pluralist solution.

The argument only works if it is actually through R*, and R* alone, that the applicability of Roman law is limited to the Roman Empire. After all, if it were some other hidden or implicit norm that effected the separation of applicability, we would be thrown back to the above solution where a universal norm U was responsible for the separation and thus the normative unification of legal systems. So, it has to be the case that without R* the applicability of Roman law would not be limited to the Roman Empire. If that is the case, however, then Roman law is in principle applicable universally, ie also including the Chinese Empire. The same is true for Chinese Imperial law. But if, from the point of view of Roman law, Roman law is applicable universally (and thus also to the Chinese Empire), then Chinese law is valid in the Chinese Empire only because Roman law, via R*, allows it be valid. So, at least from the point of view of Roman law, C is valid only because it is allowed to be valid, ie it is valid only because of R*.

Hence, if we took the limitation of applicability of Roman law to the Roman Empire to be an effect not of a superior universal norm U but of a Roman norm R*, then the result would not be a pluralistic one but, rather, that any law whatsoever would be delegated by this norm R*, thus unifying all law into one system. A norm cannot meaningfully limit a competence it does not possess, and in order to allot competences it has to possess the competence to allot competences. So, if R* is to limit the applicability of R to the Roman Empire, R* must have the competence over any law whatsoever and C can apply to the Chinese Empire only because R* allows it to apply there. The same is, of course, true from the point of view of Chinese Imperial law. Whatever point of view one takes, one always ends up with a monistic construction and never with a pluralistic one. One can never take both points of view at the same time. This is not a contingent empirical fact about the set-up of our world, but a necessary logical fact about the nature and operation of legal rules.

The final riposte bites the bullet and accepts that monism is necessary true. What it claims, however, is that the victory of monism is a Pyrrhic victory: monism has been saved at the cost of making it trivial, uninteresting or even tautologically true.

This, however, is thinking too quickly. It assumes that everything that is necessarily true is also trivially true—which is certainly not the case. It is necessarily true that the three angles in a triangle add up to 180 degrees. Whilst necessarily being true, it is certainly not trivially true. It is worth telling people and, if people deny it, it is worth demonstrating. There are, of course, many truths of this kind.[10] Whether a necessary truth is interesting or not depends not only on its own necessity, but also on what beliefs tend to be held as plausible.

So what does the necessary 'legal relation' between all norms actually signify? Let us start by making clear what it certainly does not mean: it does not mean that all law forms one legal system in a sociological or otherwise cultural sense. It would be absurd to deny that there are different legal cultures, and certainly French law is not British law. The argument about monism is not about legal culture. Legal culture and the unity of a legal system run

---

[10] Many examples for necessary yet interesting truths can be found in R Sorensen, *Thought Experiments* (Oxford, Oxford University Press, 1998).

perpendicularly. Just as monism does not necessitate a unitary legal culture, so different legal cultures do not necessitate different legal systems, as can plainly be seen in the case of federal states: the different US states, for example, all have different legal histories and cultures, yet they are all undeniably part of one legal system.

The young Kelsen believed that the necessary unity of the law amounts to the demand of material consistency of all law, ie ultimately the demand that R and C do not conflict. He tied up his version of legal monism so tightly with this demand for material consistency that when he later gave up the demand for material consistency he also felt compelled to jettison monism.[11] But I think that Kelsen was rushing through things here. Whilst the older Kelsen might very well have been right that demanding material consistency puts too much of a burden on the positive law, legal monism is independent from the claim for material consistency and thus survives even if we let go of the latter.

So if it is neither a degree of cultural homogeneity nor material consistency, what does 'legal relation' signify? If it is not the case that they must not contradict each other, in what sense are R and C 'necessarily related' if they are both to be considered legally valid? They are related in the sense that there has to be some kind of legal procedure to determine how to apply both rules and how to deal with potential legal conflict. This procedure can be 'apply the younger rule', 'apply the rule which is geographically applicable', 'apply the higher rule and disregard the lower rule' or 'apply the rule you think is better'. It does not matter what the procedure is, but it has to give both rules consideration. Consideration here means that both norms are worth discursive reflection and that no legal rule can be excluded from the outset without giving legal reasons for this exclusion. Of course, in many cases, as in our example of the two empires, these legal reasons are so obvious that they do not need much elaboration. Whilst it is certainly an obvious fact that Roman law is not to be applied in the Chinese Empire and vice versa, it is no less a legal fact.

One corollary of this is further specified by Vinx: monism is the claim that all legal conflicts are amenable to legal resolutions, whereas pluralism must certainly claim that inter-systemic conflicts have no legal resolution but are—in a Schmittian sense—irreducibly political.[12]

III. NORMATIVE MONISM

The step from legal monism to normative monism is a small one: one needs only to follow through the above line of argument and drop the qualification

---

[11] See H Kelsen, *General Theory of Norms* (Oxford, Clarendon Press, 1991) 214.
[12] Vinx, 'The Kelsen–Hart Debate' (n 3), 81.

'legal'. The argument I present will thus not rely on meta-ethical reflections on the nature and status of 'ought' statements. Rather, it will trace the same formal route we went down in order to argue for legal monism:[13] any establishment of two or more separated normative realms implicitly relies on a norm of separation. Such a norm of separation unifies the realms it is supposed to separate.

Before laying out this argument in more detail, let me make a couple of clarifications: normative monism must be kept conceptually separate from value monism, with which it is not conceptually tied up and to which it is not committed. Normative monism is thus not opposed to value pluralism.[14] Conversely, normative monism might very well be a constitutive element of a sound value-pluralist theory. The reason for this comes to light as soon as one acknowledges that any theory of a pluralism of values has to account for the fact that plural, incommensurable or incomparable values still have to be intelligible as values. The normative monist can tell a story of how a single normative space, whilst not committing us to any substantive notions of axiological consistency or comparability, nevertheless prestructures the argumentative landscape. As we will see later on, normative monism, just like legal monism, is a thin formal claim, and whilst it is certainly theoretically interesting and practically relevant, it does not commit one to either material consistency or universal comparability of values. Equally, normative monism does not deny that there might be different or distinguishable sources of normativity. All it claims is that all these sources lead into one sea of normativity.

Given all these caveats, I do not think that normative monism is a particularly controversial position to hold. It is simply the insight that we as agents and addressees of normative claims are in an important sense unitary, that reason is in an important sense unitary and that, in this respect, the topological nature of normativity has to reflect this quality of ours. Normative monism is but the elaboration of what Thomas Nagel calls the 'singleness of decision'.[15] This insight is, I think, also what drives natural law theory to deny that there can be a legal ought which is strictly separable from the moral ought yet at the same time is normatively sound and not reducible to prudential considerations.[16]

---

[13] By going down this route I follow Kelsen's instructive lead to model solutions to meta-ethical questions on legal structures and not vice versa.

[14] For a good starting point to the discussion, see C Heathwood, 'Monism and Pluralism about Value' in I Hirose et al (eds), *The Oxford Handbook of Value Theory* (Oxford, Oxford University Press, 2015) 136.

[15] T Nagel, *Mortal Questions* (Cambridge, Cambridge University Press, 1979) ch 9. Nagel is right to argue that we cannot deduce from the singleness of decision the necessity of a unified theory of how to decide. But what we undoubtedly do get from this irreducible singleness is the weaker claim that there is only one normativity.

[16] Finnis, for instance, calls the 'moralist' the 'reasonable person with unrestricted perspective': J Finnis, *Natural Law and Natural Rights*, 2nd edn (Oxford, Oxford University Press, 2011) 361.

It inspires many forms of contemporary hard positivism and can, I think, be considered a mainstream view in meta-ethics.[17]

Despite all of this, common sense suggests that normative monism is plainly wrong: after all, morality, law, etiquette and, say, the rules of chess seem quite straightforwardly to inhabit distinct and separate islands of normativity. They do not seem to form one normative system.

However, just as in the case of legal normativity, we can only consider all of these systems to be normatively valid simultaneously if we at the same time presuppose the validity of an application regime, which either distributes different realms of application to each normative realm or which resolves overlapping realms of application by means of a priority rule.

Let us look at the relation between morality and, say, chess. A normative pluralist would claim that, at its core, the rules of chess and the rules of morality are different and separable sets of rules. Both apply to different spheres of human life and are thus separate normative realms. However, as we have seen in the discussion of legal monism, such a normative separation of spheres of application quite straightforwardly establishes monism rather than pluralism: if there are to be different spheres of applicability, different competences for the different normative realms, there has to be some kind of allocation of applicability, some kind of rule X that determines the field of competence of each realm. This rule, in turn, unifies the two normative systems.

Now, morality is widely held to be both comprehensive and dominant, ie it is held to be in principle relevant to all decisions and, where relevant, to defeat all other considerations.[18] Thus, for most moral philosophers, this allocation rule X is part of morality.

So, usually, the chess/morality system in seen in the following way: morality applies to all circumstances and defeats all other considerations. However, some actions are morally neutral, like the act of pushing pieces across a board. Such acts can be governed by other sets of rules, eg the rules of chess. This division of spheres of competences is an effect of morality itself. Because of comprehensiveness and dominance, it is morality that allocates all other competences, and this competence-competence resides within morality.

---

[17] See J Jarvis Thomson, 'Normativity' in R Shafer-Landau (ed), *Oxford Studies in Metaethics*, vol 2 (Oxford, Oxford University Press, 2007) 240, who rejects the view that there are multiple senses of ought, each related to a different normative domain, and thus rejects the idea that there was a different legal ought, to be distinguished from a moral ought and from an ought of courtesy or chess.

[18] Apart from 'political realists', who reject the comprehensiveness, and 'dirty hand theorists', who reject the dominance of morality, I think it is safe to say that most moral philosophers are implicitly committed to comprehensiveness and dominance. See CAJ Coady, 'The Moral Reality in Realism' (2005) 22 *Journal of Applied Philosophy* 121.

The normative competence of all other normative fields is delegated by morality. The rules of chess apply as long as they do not violate morality, so you may promote your pawn to queen by advancing it to the last row if this does not, by some awful coincidence or devilish interference, mean that someone innocent gets killed. But as long as you do not violate morality, the chess rules can legislate whatever they want. Under this construction, it is plain that one ends up with only one normative system, which could be called the empire of morality, or perhaps the kingdom of ends. All other seemingly separate normative realms are dependent territories of this kingdom.

There is thus a sense in which chess and morality are two different normative systems. A normative monist would not deny that—just as a legal monist would not deny that there is a sense in which French and German law are different legal systems. What a normative monist does deny is that it could ever be the case that there was no normative relation between chess and morality. This is inconceivable, since the more clearly the spheres of applicability of the two systems are separated, the more clearly the two systems are related via the requisite norm of separation.

To be sure, monism does not depend on the comprehensiveness and dominance of morality. If we truly held that there were some areas to which morality did not apply, or that there were matters on which, even if it did apply, it did not have the last word, then there would still have to be an allocation rule X, which, whilst not part of morality, would still determine which norms apply where.

Normative monism, too, is thus a necessary result and not a contingent fact about the set-up of our normative systems. But is it interesting? As we have seen, normative monism does not lead to or favour value monism. Nor does it favour moral comprehensiveness or dominance over more politically realistic constructions. Equally, it does not commit one to normative uniformity or homogeneity of content. So what does it commit one to?

Well, normative monism tells us some crucial information about the nature of the normative space as such. It tells us at least three crucial things: (i) no valid norm can be excluded as irrelevant a priori. Thus, (ii) all valid norms are in principle normatively reachable from any point in the normative space and (iii) all normative considerations are in principle relevant to each other. Special reasons need to be given to exclude a valid norm as irrelevant, and those special reasons have to have the form of norms. The normative space is thus a continuous space that does have loopholes or inaccessible areas. These are topological qualities, which we can call non-exclusion, reachability and continuity.

As merely topological qualities of the normative space, these might seem to be entirely abstract qualities. However, as it will turn out, they are highly relevant to the relation of law and morality.

IV. THE GREAT INCOMPATIBILITY

Where do we stand? I have argued that, by necessity, there can only ever be one continuous normative system. Thus, in order to be valid simultaneously, law and morality would have to be part of a single normative system. In this conditional claim lies the truth and one of the main insights of natural law theory: if law and morality are to be simultaneously valid, they have to be part of one normative system.

The problem is that law and morality cannot be part of one normative system. Therefore, they cannot be valid simultaneously.

Why should this be the case? Have we not seen above that morality and, say, chess can quite easily be understood as being part of one normative system? Why should this be different for the law?

There are two lines of argument offered by the Pure Theory to the effect that law and morality cannot form part of one and the same normative system. One is the classic, if ill explored, argument advanced by Kelsen himself, roughly arguing that the dynamic nature of the law makes it incompatible with a static system like morality. The other is an argument flowing from the wider reading of the Pure Theory and made explicit most clearly by Fichte, namely that the law as a system of permissions is incompatible with morality as a system of duties, or, put more precisely, that the law as a system of conditional normativity is incompatible with morality as a system of unconditional normativity. Both arguments, as I hope to be able to show, are related and ultimately rest on the same insight about the law. Since the argument taken from the wider reading of the Pure Theory is both the more unfamiliar and the more basic one, I will start with this argument first.

Remember the Fichte quote I gave above:

> A right is something that one can avail oneself of or not. Thus a right follows from a merely permissive law, and it is a permissive law because it is limited only to a certain sphere, from which it can be inferred that outside the sphere of the law one is free from it, and if there is no other law concerning the object, one is generally left solely to one's own arbitrary will. This permission is not explicitly contained in the law; it is merely inferred from an interpretation of the law, from its limited character. The limited character of law manifests itself in the fact that it is conditioned. It is absolutely impossible to see how a permissive law should be derivable from the moral law, which commands unconditionally and thereby extends its reach to everything.[19]

The fact that Fichte is couching his analysis in rights talk should not concern us here as it is not a necessary feature of the structure he is highlighting.

---

[19] JG Fichte, *Foundations of Natural Right*, ed F Neuhouser, trans M Baur (Cambridge, Cambridge University Press, 2000) 14.

What is relevant is that the law is limited or conditioned in character and that this distinguishes it from morality, which is not so limited or conditioned. This, Fichte argues, leads to the absolute impossibility of deriving the law from morality. In what follows, I want to further defend and expand on this Fichtean claim of the principled underivability of the law from morality and also make clear why this underivability necessarily leads to the incompatibility between law and morality which is the basis of the normative jinx.

Fichte expands on the above discussion thus:

> The answer is: all this necessarily follows if the law prescribes a determinate sphere for itself, if it directly carries within itself the quantity of its own validity. As soon as the law indicates the sphere to which it applies, it thereby simultaneously determines the sphere to which it does not apply; it explicitly holds itself back from anything about this sphere and making prescriptions with respect to it.—In relation to a particular person, I am absolved from adhering to the law requiring me to treat him as a free being, and the question of how I will treat him depends solely upon my free choice, or I have a right of coercion against him. These claims mean, and can mean, nothing other than: this person cannot, through the law of right alone, prevent my coercion of him (although he may well do so through other laws, by physical strength, or by appealing to the moral law). My coercion is not contrary to this law, and if the other person has nothing to appeal to by it, he must endure my coercion of him.[20]

What is Fichte driving at? He is referring to the following difficulty: the law sets down certain conditions under which the use of force is permitted. Now, for Fichte, the permission is not the result of a particular action of the law but is a structural feature of the law in so far as it flows from the very conditioned nature of the law. In setting down or carrying within itself criteria of where it applies, the law also sets down or carries within itself criteria of where it does not apply. In those spaces which it leaves out, where it does not apply, the law remains silent and allows people to do what they want, including the use of force. The fact that the law is issuing permissions and permitting the use of force, Fichte claims, does not flow not from any specific content of the law but from the very way the law applies: it issues permissions by its very nature of being limited. Its distinction from morality is not comprehensive in the sense of offering a moral reason that speaks in favour of or against any given act or state of affairs.[21] Rather, there are fields where the law is fully silent, where it

---

[20] ibid 83.

[21] Value pluralism denies this feature of morality. However, it ends up struggling with this denial: value pluralism can only make sense if there are no moral reasons to prefer one value over the other. This, though, would make most of the decisions which we feel are the most important and morally pregnant decisions in our lives unreasonable in the sense that we could just as well have flipped a coin. Furthermore, there is more to morality than just value—for example, the interests of others. Finally, value pluralism faces a classic dilemma: either it has a

has nothing to say. According to Fichte, the law permits the use of force, it is coercive, by being silent. I described the law's operation in terms of the law declaring the use of force 'lawful'. Fichte tried to get to the basis and foundation of the law by focusing on the silence of the law and the ensuing permission to use force in this area. I think these two approaches are alternative ways to express the same idea.

Take the way in which ancient Germanic law regulated murder. The Germans only had one rule that dealt with murder:[22]

(7)   Everyone who kills a member of our tribe loses his membership in our tribe.

The law is silent about someone killing a non-member. So, whilst the killing of a member is unlawful, the killing of a non-member is not unlawful and is thus permitted. The permission is a result of the conditional nature of the law in the sense that rule (7) only provides a legal result (loss of membership) for specific acts and not for others. It has a clear sphere of applicability in that it applies only to killings of members of our tribe. These other acts, then, are permitted in a legal sense. This permission is a result of the limited or conditional nature of the law.

The law thus indirectly permits the acts to which it does not refer. It indirectly refers to a certain sphere of the world, produces a legal consequence in this sphere and so, in a sense, includes it by not referring to it. The law is in a sense overly comprehensive: it includes the sphere that it does not include by excluding it. This is not meant to be a puzzling or paradoxical claim: the law 'legally allows' acts by not referring to them at all. Morality, conversely, is comprehensive in a conventional sense. It includes any act by including it, it allows things by referring to them. Since morality is full reason, and since reason can be applied to everything, no decision is truly morally irrelevant. Whether I put on a blue or a yellow shirt, whether I buy Colgate or Crest, might be economically or aesthetically irrelevant, but it can never be fully morally irrelevant given that the colour of my shirt or choice of toothpaste will have an effect on other people, will, even if minimally, affect their lives and will thus be of moral relevance. Of course, it might very well be the case, as value-pluralists argue, that different

---

reasonable principle that allows us to distinguish value from un-value, which makes it hard to see why the principle could not be reformulated as a super-value, or it does not have a reasonable principle to distinguish value from un-value, in which case the entire list of values would appear to be an arbitrary stipulation.

[22] B Rehfeldt, 'Die Vergeistigung des Rechtes. Zur Frage der Gesetzmäßigkeiten der Rechtsentwicklung' (1950) 67 *Zeitschrift der Savigny-Stiftung für Rechtsgeschichte. Germanische Abteilung* 373, 380. 'There exists permitted murder. Only the one not permitted is a violation of the law': H Brunner and CF von Schwerin, *Deutsche Rechtsgeschichte. Band II*, 2nd edn (Berlin, Duncker und Humboldt 1928) 816.

but valuable courses of action are incomparable and incommensurable, and that a choice between them is rationally underdetermined. So, in terms of value, I might not change anything in my life if I consider myself a Crest guy rather than a Colgate guy. However, a moral analysis does not stop there. After all, I might affect the life of a morally deserving factory worker in a morally significant way by contributing to either his or another's livelihood. For morality, no fact is excluded in principle from having a moral weight, albeit a very small weight, and thus from contributing to the overall moral assessment of the situation. Morality deals with intensive quanta, with 'more or less', and its space is a deep space of gradations of intensity. Things might seem morally neutral at first glance, but if one takes into account all the possible moral repercussions of an assessed course of action, one will find that no course of action is fully morally neutral. The law, conversely, either speaks or is silent. It does not deal in intensive quanta, but only in extensive ones. Its space is flat. This means that the law either fully applies or does not apply at all. If it applies, it determines the legal consequences. If it does not apply, it permits any course of action. So, if the law is silent about which shirt to put on or which toothpaste to buy, then, from a legal perspective, there is really no legal consideration to be had whatsoever and I am allowed to do as I please.

But is this difference in the mode of application enough to get to the 'absolute impossibility' of deriving any law whatsoever from morality that Fichte was speaking of? Could not the law be taken to give at least a broad-brush rendering of the moral picture or a two-dimensional projection of the moral space? I do not think it can, and even if it could, it would not change much. First of all, I do not think that morality produces a traceable outline, but rather an infinite amount of such traceable outlines. In its world of principles, rules, exceptions, reasons, defeasible reasons, values, duties and so on, φ-ing might be morally commanded if k, but not if k and l; it might again if k, l and m, but not if k, l, m and n; and so on. Furthermore, we might not yet know of reasons o, p and q and might not have considered what they mean for φ-ing. The fact that we have not considered them, however, does not mean that these reasons do not apply. Hence, from the point of view of morality, we can 'zoom' into the moral consideration of any action and see the moral results oscillate depending on the depth of reasons we consider. Because the moral space is deep, morality looks different at every different level of depth. Since the law cannot convey this depth, it could only ever trace one of those myriad cross-sections, which by definition cannot give the 'moral' picture. Of course, the law also knows the discontinuous logic of defeasability.[23] However, this

---

[23] JF Beltrán and GB Ratti (eds), *The Logic of Legal Requirements. Essays on Defeasibility* (Oxford, Oxford University Press, 2012).

legal defeasability is a contingent feature limited and predetermined by the given content of the law. In morality, it is part of the very structure of moral thought.

But why should this non-derivability of law from morality imply the incompatibility of law and morality? Why should the fact that law cannot be derived from morality make it impossible that law and morality are part of one and the same normative system? Given the correctness of the analysis above, from the morality point of view, the law must necessarily seem immoral. After all, the law operates by being entirely silent about certain acts described externally. It does not declare that, all things considered, certain acts are permitted; rather, it permits these acts by not even considering them. The law does not allow the killing of someone who has killed a member of our tribe by arguing that this person deserves to be killed or, for that matter, by adducing any reasons whatsoever. Rather, it solves the issue by not even considering the case where someone is killed who is not a member of our tribe. This case remains outside of the law's consideration and is thus allowed. Now this lack of consideration is essential to the operation of the law as law yet is at the same time anathema to moral reflection, which consists in giving everything full consideration. Thus, it is not only that the content of the law can at times appear immoral—it is the entire operation of the law that is immoral. So, even if we had a law that tried to be perfectly moral, it could not be perfectly moral whilst still remaining law. This fact will be further explored in the second argument in favour of the incompatibilism thesis below. However, if the law is in its very nature immoral, it is hard to see how law and morality could be part of one normative system.

There is another, maybe less esoteric, reason why law and morality cannot be part of one and the same normative system and thus cannot be considered to be valid at the same time. This reason has been put forward by Hans Kelsen himself, but has so far not receive the attention I think it deserves. It mainly consists in arguing that what distinguishes law from chess is that whilst chess, just as morality, is a static normative system, the law is a dynamic normative system. This means that the law has a different mode of individuating or applying its content: whilst the content of rules of morality and chess are individuated or applied by way of thought or reflection, the law's content is individuated and applied by way of decisions, or acts of will. This difference in content individuation, taken together with the topological quality of the continuity of the normative space, produces the normative jinx.

Of course, we must not overplay the difference between static and dynamic, just as we must not overplay the difference between thinking and willing. Each act of thought is certainly also an act of will, and no act of will can be entirely devoid of thought. Whatever the actual and spurious differences between thinking and willing—and they have been discussed in the literature *ad nauseam*—I will rely on a simple example to illustrate one decisive and irreducible difference between the static and dynamic modes of content individuation: in the law, it is possible, and also quite common, that a legally faulty and thus wrong decision, which is known to be faulty and wrong, nonetheless becomes part of the law. This could be the case, for instance, when a faulty court judgment or an unconstitutional statute is, for whatever reason, not challenged legally.[24] It is quite common for even unlawful law to become law. This is an effect of what in German is called *Rechtskraft*. The idea is conveyed in the English language by the concepts of legal force, preclusion, collateral estoppel and *res judicata*.[25]

Such an effect would be inconceivable in the realm of morality. In morality, what is known to be in violation of morality cannot be part of morality. No moral rule could ever remain part of the stock of moral rules if everyone knew that it was a morally wrong rule. It would be inconceivable because it is essential to the point of morality to exclude precisely this kind of content.[26]

This, however, is not the case with the law. It is certainly not essential to the point of the law that it should prevent itself from having a certain content.

This fundamental and irreducible difference results from the privileged role the decision plays in the positive law. Whatever its supposed content, the law by necessity authorises the creation of law in violation of this content.[27]

But what does this mean for the relation of law and morality? It means that the standard way the relation of law and morality is modelled is flawed. With some minor differences, both contemporary legal positivists and natural law theorists agree that it is best to model the morality/law relation along the lines

[24] For a discussion of this topic, which is generally neglected in the Anglo-American literature, see A Merkl, *Die Lehre von der Rechtskraft: Entwickelt aus dem Rechtsbegriff. Eine rechtstheoretische Untersuchung* (Vienna, Deuticke 1923). See also C Kletzer, 'Kelsen's Development of the *Fehlerkalkül*-Theory' (2005) 18 *Ratio Juris* 46.

[25] It is also a frequent feature of quick, competitive games that decisions of referees which later turn out to be factually wrong (eg a throw in was given even though the ball did not cross the touchline) remain unchallengeable and thus become part of the official score. Whilst there is, of course, a certain analogy to the doctrine of *res judicata*, the analogy only goes that far. The decisive difference of such unchallengeable refereeing decisions to the dynamic system of the law is that such decisions only relate to factual errors and not to the erroneous understanding of the rules of football themselves or to the creation of such rules.

[26] Of course, some argue that in morality there is a 'right to do wrong', but this is a different matter altogether. It does not arise from the individuation of a general moral norm in violation of this general norm, but is an alleged feature of moral rights. See J Waldron, 'A Right to Do Wrong' (1981) 92 *Ethics* 21; WA Galston, 'On the Alleged Right to Do Wrong: A Response to Waldron' (1983) 93 *Ethics* 320; O Herstein, 'Defending the Right to Do Wrong' [2012] *Cornell Law Faculty Publications*, paper 339.

[27] It would be a mistake to conclude that this authorisation to also create law *ultra vires* is the same as the renunciation of the notion of delegation as such. After all, the fact that there might be two routes to the validity of a norm does not mean that there is no difference between the two routes.

of the morality/chess relation: morality sets the boundaries of what we ought and ought not to do, what we have reason to do and what we have reason not to do. Within those boundaries, we might find it hard to know exactly which reasons apply to us and/or we might not be able to unilaterally solve certain coordination problems. This is where the law is seen to step in. Roughly speaking, it is taken to add *determinationes* (concretisations, implementations)[28] to the rough grid of morality.

Now, despite its appeal, this model is, unfortunately, untenable when it comes to the relation of morality and law. This is because, in aiming to delegate to the law, morality is caught up in a quandary: it aims to hand out a materially limited competence, but it also wants to hand it out to a system that does not fully respect material constraint, a system into which this material constraint does not directly translate. So, in this delegation to the law, morality is either not in earnest with material constraint or it is not in earnest with the delegation itself. As soon as morality allows for law, it by necessity allows for the possibility of creation of law in violation of morality. This is the simple consequence of the doctrine of legal force. Allowing for law and allowing for the violation of morality thus mean one and the same thing.

This means that as soon as morality delegates to the law, it delegates to a system where the wrong can become the right. So, as soon as morality delegates to the law, it cannot contain the delegation. This is why Kelsen writes that 'the delegation of positive by natural law must mean that natural law empowers positive law to replace it'.[29]

There are two classic strategies to try to avoid this conclusion. One is to deny outright the necessarily dynamic character of the law. The other is to accept the dynamic character of the law but to claim that morality can retain mastery of the terms of the delegation and thus contain the dynamism of the law.

The first strategy is the one followed, at least in part, by Dworkin's interpretivism. It argues that the law is dynamic only in a pre-interpretative sense. In a full post-interpretative sense, the law is ultimately not dependent on will or decision, but only on sound moral reason.[30] Thus, whilst unlawful and

---

[28] Finnis (n 16) 284; Aquinas, Summa Theologica, 1a2ae. 91,3.

[29] Kelsen, *General Theory of Law and State* (n 2) 413.

[30] Dworkin stresses that law in the full post-interpretative sense depends on the data of the practices that are being interpreted, so it depends on will and decision, and not only on sound moral reason. However, whenever moral appeal comes into conflict with fit, it seems that for Dworkin moral appeal wins: 'It is conceivable, for example, that though the officials of a particular legal system all assumed, in good faith, that on the best understanding their law authorized capital punishment for murder, they were all wrong in that belief. I myself take that view, in fact, of the situation in many states of the United States now. I think that no American state's law, properly understood, actually authorizes capital punishment because such punishment is unconstitutional under the Eighth Amendment of the United States Constitution, in spite of the

immoral law might be part of the law in a pre-interpretative sense, it is not part of the law in the full sense of the term. This solution is certainly not without merits. However, as has been commented,[31] it comes at a very high theoretical price: it requires us to introduce a theoretically difficult dichotomy at the heart of our concept of law, and it requires us to give up the doctrine of *res judicata* in relation to law in the full sense of the term.

The second strategy is the classic natural law strategy. It argues that morality remains firmly in the driving seat regarding the delegation of individuation to the positive law. Finnis, for instance, claims against Kelsen that 'to delegate is not to delegate unconditionally'.[32]

This is true. The question, however, is whether conditional delegation of powers to the law is at all possible in the way Finnis envisages.

The material conditioning of the delegation of powers according to Finnis rests on a complex rider and is further complicated by the collateral duty one has to obey laws which, taken by themselves, have actually overstepped this material limitation. However complicated and meandering, Finnis thinks that there is a line that can be drawn between what the law can do and what it cannot do.[33]

The problem lies not so much in the specific design of the line drawn, but in its very nature. The difficulty resides not so much in conditions of delegation, but in the very nature of 'conditional delegation'.

How is conditional delegation supposed to work? There are two ways of modelling conditional delegation which are usually run together: (i) the idea that the conditions of delegation do not translate into legal conditions but remain purely moral conditions; and (ii) the idea that the conditions of delegation translate into the law and thereby become legal conditions.

---

fact that the Supreme Court, which once did take the same view, has since changed its mind and said that capital punishment, in some circumstances, is validly authorized by state law after all.' R Dworkin, 'Hart's Posthumous Reply' (2017) 130 *Harvard Law Review* 2096, 2099–2100. Whilst it may be morally appealing to interpret the Supreme Court's ruling to mean that capital punishment cannot be authorised by state law, it is certainly not fitting with what the Supreme Court has actually ruled. For Dworkin, the moral appeal here trumps the fit with the past practice of a quite clear declaration of the Supreme Court.

[31] See A Marmor, *Interpretation and Legal Theory* (Oxford, Hart Publishing, 2005) 27–47; J Raz, *Ethics in the Public Domain: Essays in the Morality of Law and Politics* (Oxford, Oxford University Press, 1995) 210, 220–26.

[32] Finnis (n 16) 27. Finnis accepts Kelsen's portrayal of natural law theory and his formulation of 'delegation' as not classical, but still accurate.

[33] Whilst Finnis keeps stressing that the question of iniquitous law is not a central question for him or for classic natural law theory, it is certainly a central question to many, and can also work as one of the few litmus tests as to where people stand in questions of legal philosophy. For Finnis, ultimately, there is a clear line to be drawn where *lex iniusta non est lex*, although such a statement must be understood as equivocating between secondary and focal senses of the word *lex*.

The problem is that neither of the two options seems to get conditional delegation right: in the first case (i), it is hard to see how emphatically non-legal conditions can condition the validity of law. Of course, any non-legal fact can become a condition for the validity of law—the raising of hands, the uttering of words and so on—but this can only work if the law declares these facts to be conditions. The non-legality of the moral conditions is not taken here as a provisional quality; rather, according to this view, it is the moral quality of these rules itself, and not a reference to this moral quality by the law, that limits the competence of the law.

There is a certain magic at work in this view, and few natural law theorists would actually argue that morality itself conditions the validity of the law.[34] Instead, what most would argue is that, whilst not directly conditioning the validity of the law, morality conditions the 'obligatoriness' of it. However, this divorce of validity and bindingness of rules, as appealing a route as it might seem to get us out of this predicament, comes at a very high cost: it divests validity of its normative nature and relegates it to the role of a mere indicator of membership. On the other hand, it overextends the notion of 'obligation', which is uprooted from its actual instantiation in valid norms and turned into a crypto-metaphysical, magical quality.[35]

Under this view, valid rules can be, but do not have to be, obligatory. Equally, it seems, non-valid rules must be able to be obligatory, as is the case with *jus cogens*. At one point, Finnis claims that validity is at least a necessary condition of obligation.[36] This, however, sits uncomfortably with his theory of *jus cogens*, the whole point of which is to be binding by virtue of its content and not of an enactment.[37]

Thus, ultimately, validity decides nothing. Equally irrelevant is the question as to whether there might be a secondary or collateral moral duty to obey (somewhat) immoral but valid laws.[38] The idea here is that validity is not irrelevant, as we have morally good reason to follow even (somewhat) morally defective laws if they are valid, since having a legal regime is itself an objective

---

[34] Robert Alexy is one of the few authors who would argue that morality conditions the validity of law. For a set of recent arguments against Finnis's account of natural law along those lines, see R Alexy, 'Some Reflections on the Ideal Dimension of Law and on the Legal Philosophy of John Finnis' (2013) 58(2) *American Journal of Jurisprudence* 97. For Finnis's reply, see J Finnis, 'Law as Fact and as Reason for Action: A Response to Robert Alexy on Law's "Ideal Dimension"' (2014) 59(1) *American Journal of Jurisprudence* 85.

[35] Finnis does not solve the problem of obligation and accepts this conclusion at end of chapter 11. He postpones the analysis to theological reflections. This should not surprise us. At least Finnis, just like Kant, is upfront about the fact that one cannot explain this kind of isolated obligation without theology. Finnis (n 16) 343.

[36] Finnis (n 16) 334.

[37] Finnis (n 34) 94–95.

[38] Finnis (n 16) 351–52 and 362. Finnis calls these obligations 'diminished' and 'extra-legal'.

good and not following these valid if (somewhat) defective laws would under-mine this legal system.

But is it really validity that makes the difference here? No. What makes all the difference is a quality that usually goes hand in hand with validity and is therefore easily confused with it: the effectiveness of rules. After all, it is not the validity of rules that gives us good moral reasons to comply with (slightly) immoral laws, but their actual effective operation.

To see that legal validity is irrelevant in arguments about collateral duties, one need only ask whether an effective rule that is for some reason formally invalid would fail to create collateral duties of this kind. Of course, it would not. But does validity not at least solve co-ordination problems? Do we not need valid rules to know which side of the road to drive on? Not really. It is, again, the effectiveness of rules and not their validity that solves the co-ordination problem.

All validity might be granted to do under this theory is to lend a defeasible presumption of obligatoriness, a prima facie obligatoriness. This, however, does not really matter here, because the only standpoint that matters is the all-things-considered standpoint, especially in cases where a full consideration is not only possible but also obligatory, as is the case in moral matters. Again, it is morality that decides.

So, if validity decides nothing and morality everything, what is the point of validity? And if there is no point to validity thus understood, in what sense should we speak of delegation at all? By first maintaining that morality itself determines the validity of the law and then divorcing validity from binding-ness, we have saved conditionality only by sacrificing delegation.

The second model (ii) of conditional delegation does not fare much better. If we translate morality's conditions into legal conditions of validity, then the problem is that the law as a dynamic system cannot be trusted with the faithful enforcement of these conditions. There is no doubt that law can be law even if it is in violation of the law. Thus, there can be no doubt that law can be law even if it is in violation of the conditions that morality has imprinted into the law. So, whilst morality *has to* understand these conditions to be absolute, the law *cannot* understand them to be such. There is thus a sense in which morality cannot imprint its conditions into the law. So, whilst delegation is possible, it is not really conditioned.[39]

---

[39] Whilst the present argument certainly gains its substance from Kelsen's reflections on the so-called *Fehlerkalkül* ('error-calculus') and alternative authorisation, it does not rely on a fully fledged defence of Kelsen's views. All it needs to get off the ground is the acceptance that there is such a thing as legal force and that it is thus at least possible that unlawful law becomes law. It could nevertheless be argued that, irrespective of voidable norms, there must still remain norms which are so far removed from their legal conditions that they are absolutely null and void. However, when one reflects on the notion of absolute nullity, one sees that here, too, someone

This structure of the dynamic individuation of content that can be found in the law is not an accidental feature of the law, ie it is not a feature that could be removed without also getting rid of the law. To demonstrate this, I will show that this feature is not just a contingent feature of complex modern legal systems where we face a complex hierarchy of norm and legal organs, but is also a necessary feature of the more primitive legal regimes I have discussed throughout the book, ie also of rules like the following:

(1)   Killing someone who has killed someone else unlawfully is lawful.

In what sense is this a dynamic rule? What we have before us here is the most simple legal system, with only three levels:

(a)   the basic norm stating that force shall be applied in accordance to the law;
(b)   the legal rule giving the conditions (X) of use of force to be lawful; and
(c)   the actual use of force.

The difference between a modern legal regime and the one instated by rule (1) is the complexity of X. In what follows, I will briefly argue that the dynamic nature of the law is not a function of this complexity but the result of the basic set-up found in (a)–(c). Even in this most primitive regime, where we have only one rule, we nevertheless have three levels of hierarchy and thus two conditionings: (b) gives the conditions of (c) being lawful and (a) gives the conditions for (b) being law. So, even in the most primitive legal system, we have the assessment of force as lawful being doubly conditioned, namely by the positive law and by the basic norm: force is lawful *if* it is in accordance with a law, which is only law *if* it is in accordance with the basic norm. Being in accordance with the basic norm here means only that the law is actually law, which means, as I discussed in chapter three, that it is real or effective, ie that it is generally used or applied as law. Now, this double conditioning is

would have to apply the criteria of absolute nullity, whatever they are, in order to decide whether the norm in question falls under them. In the case of absolute nullity, it could be argued that everyone is called upon to make this decision for themselves. In that case, the question arises whether this decision of each and every one is of a declaratory or constitutive nature. Since understanding such decisions as merely declaratory does not make sense, they have to be understood to be constitutive. This, in turn, means that until such a decision is taken, the norm is valid, and it remains valid in case the decision is never taken. Thus, there is really no place for absolute nullity. For an elaboration of this argument see Kletzer (n 24). For a discussion of Kelsen's position on alternative authorisation, see S Paulson, 'Material and Formal Authorisation in Kelsen's Pure Theory' (1980) 39 *CLJ* 172; JW Harris, 'Kelsen's Concept of Authority' (1977) 36 *CLJ* 353; D Dyzenhaus, *Legality and Legitimacy. Carl Schmitt, H Kelsen, and Hermann Heller in Weimar* (Oxford, Oxford University Press, 1997) 155; CS Nino, 'Some Confusions Surrounding Kelsen's Concept of Validity' in SL Paulson and B Litschewski-Paulson (eds), *Normativity and Norms: Critical Perspectives on Kelsenian Themes* (Oxford, Oxford University Press, 1998) 253.

what establishes the dynamic nature of the law and what makes a conditional delegation impossible. To see this, one needs to carefully attend to where morality would aim to come into the picture, ie where its conditional delegation would claim to attach to. Morality could certainly aim to directly assess (c). Then, however, it would be in direct competition with the law over the assessment of facts. Morality would not assess the law and it would not conditionally delegate to the law how to assess facts, but it would replace the law's assessment of facts. Seen this way, there would be no law left for morality.

In order to assess the law and conditionally delegate to the law without replacing it, the law would thus have to aim to assess (b). But then it would compete with (a). Now, the problem is that (a) is the description of positive or actual law, ie law that exists as opposed to law that is merely imagined. So morality can only attempt to assess the law as law if it thereby presents a different standard to (a) for identifying what counts as law. This, however, is impossible. At this level, morality does not compete with the law in its assessment of legal facts, but it competes with legal philosophy itself. In assessing (b), it could thus either fully align with (a), and thus cease to be a moral assessment, or it could replace (a) with its own criteria, in which case there would be no (b) left to assess, since the existence of (b) is conditioned by (a).

Finally, morality could try to assess (a). In that case, however, it would not assess any substantive conditions of the legality of the use of force at all. It would assess not the law, but legality, ie the fact that the law declares certain uses of force lawful. Irrespective of whether such an assessment is possible or has a point, it is certainly not what is aimed at by conditional delegation, namely, the assessment and delegation of the content of law, of X.

Morality could conceivably become part of this content of the law, it could be part of the conditions X to assess the legality of the use of force, in case, say, the legal rule applied was that only a minimally moral use of force was lawful. In this case, however, morality would only *happen to be* part of the law, ie the fact of it being a condition would itself be conditioned by (a). Conditioned morality, however, is no morality at all; it would just be content. The point of morality, conversely, is not simply to provide any kind of content which under certain conditions has certain consequences. It is to provide an unconditioned content, ie to tell an end story how to assess. Morality thus can enter the law only by turning into positive morality, ie by ceasing to be morality.

V. THE NORMATIVE JINX

In a nutshell, the argument I have presented and defended is as follows: the way that natural law theory conceptualises the relation of law and morality is the only possible way to conceptualise the relation of law and morality—but, unfortunately, natural law is in itself impossible. Put differently: natural law is correct in arguing that if law and morality claim to be both valid, they need to be part of one normative system; however, natural law is wrong in assuming that law and morality can ever be part of one normative system.

This means the following: as soon as we take the point of view of law, there is no morality to assess the law; and as soon as we take the point of view of morality, there is no law to be assessed. You can take one point of view and I can take the other. I can take one now and the other tomorrow, or I can switch back and forth between them in moments. What I cannot do is take both at the same time.

However much we would like to have an object of assessment when we talk morally about the law, we simply do not have one. As soon as we try to assess the law morally, what we are assessing cannot possibly be the law. What we are assessing are thus social arrangements, constellations of influence, modes of force and coercion, and the like. It is certainly morally wrong to incentivise people to kill each other, to coerce them to keep racially segregated and so on. However, as soon as one employs this moral filter, there is no valid law to assess. What is left are only acts of force and coercion. If, on the other hand, one takes the legal perspective and argues that one really ought to pay taxes, that one really is allowed to kill someone in self-defence etc, then there is no morality left from which to assess these claims.

The normative jinx might be a surprising result, but it follows neatly from what are, I think, rather uncontroversial claims. It plays a rather important role in the specific understanding of the law presented in this book. I argued in the previous chapters that the law is primarily an order of force or violence in the sense that it orders force by declaring its use lawful. The demands issued by the law, such as 'drive on this side of the road', 'pay your taxes' and 'do not steal', are norms that the law issues by means of declaring certain occurrences of force lawful. Not only are these demands secondary in relation to the primary permission of force, but they are, just as the permissions to use force themselves, in a sense inaccessible to moral assessment due to the normative jinx described here.

For the Pure Theory, the problem with respect to the relation of law and morality is thus that law and morality both want to do the same thing in a different and ultimately incompatible way.

Kelsen, for instance, stressed that the positive law is 'ethical-political speculation',[40] that it is an ideology[41] and that the law itself is a relative morality.[42]

---

[40] H Kelsen, *Der soziologische und der juristische Staatsbegriff. Kritische Untersuchung des Verhältnisses von Staat und Recht* (Vienna, Deuticke 1928), 46.

[41] H Kelsen, *The Pure Theory of Law*, 2nd edn, trans M Knight (Berkeley, University of California Press, 1967) 104–105.

[42] ibid 65.

This view is, of course, not new. Hegel, for instance, claimed that the law shares its content with ethical institutions like positive morality, churches, the family and so on:[43] 'It is philosophical insight which recognises that Church and state are not opposed to each other as far as their *content* is concerned, which is truth and rationality, but merely differ in *form*.'

What sets it apart from those institutions and what produces the normative jinx is not the content of the law, but its form:

> In contrast with the *faith* and *authority* of the Church in relation to ethics, rights, laws, and institutions, and with its *subjective conviction*, the state possesses *knowledge*. Within its principle, the content in no longer essentially confined to the form of feeling and faith, but belongs to determinate thought.

This is of crucial importance. It is not the content, which distinguishes the law from morality, but only its form. 'The question about the relationship between law and morals is not a question about the content of the law, but one about its form.'[44] As we have seen, what differentiates the law from morality is that the system of schemata of interpretation which structures the law does it procedurally, whereas morality lacks this procedural quality. Procedurally here means that the law is doubly conditioned.

The legal moralist is deluded by the fact that the law often happens to have the same content as the moral enterprise and falsely concludes from this that the law can learn something from morality. He misses the crucial point that the law is of a different form: 'Since morality always evaluates actuality, a moral evaluation of the positive law directly only relates to the acts which create norms, and it relates to the norms themselves only indirectly.'[45]

Whenever we think we are morally evaluating 'the law', what we are actually evaluating is a specific act of creation of law. Claiming that a certain statute is morally reprehensible is shorthand for saying that Parliament should not have enacted this statute. This, however, means the following: morality and the law both assess the same goings-on (eg in a room a majority of the people stand up and say 'Aye' after a text is read) differently. Whilst morality deems that they should not have happened and that they should thus not have any consequences, the law deems that they mean that a certain statute is created and that they thus will have consequences.

Morality cannot assess the law because law and morality compete over the assessment of the same goings-on. Put differently: since the law is created

---

[43] GWF Hegel, *Elements of the Philosophy of Right*, trans HB Nisbet (Cambridge, Cambridge University Press, 1991) 299, §270 Addition. Original emphasis.

[44] Kelsen (n 41) 65.

[45] H Kelsen, *Reine Rechtslehre*, 2nd edn (Vienna, Deuticke, 1967) 69. The quote is taken from a footnote in the German original which has been omitted in the English translation.

by the legal assessment of facts, the moral assessment of the law becomes impossible since it could only either leave the legal assessment intact (in which case it would be pointless as it would make no difference) or it would replace the legal assessment (in which case we would have no law left, since the law is created only by the legal assessment of facts).

The problem thus is not simply that law and morality are conceptually unrelated, but that they are related in a way which reveals the strict impossibility of a moral treatment of 'the law'. As 'the law' itself is not a thing, but a relation of norms and facts, as it is an 'assessment' of facts, it is not a suitable object of moral assessment: 'From the point of view of positive law as a system of valid norms, morality does not exist as such.'[46]

---

[46] H Kelsen, *General Theory of Law and State* (n 2) 374; HLA Hart, 'Kelsen Visited' in B Litschewski Paulson and SL Paulson (eds), *Normativity and Norms. Critical Perspectives on Kelsenian Themes* (Oxford, Oxford University Press, 1998) 83.

7

Absolute Positivism

I. INTRODUCTION

IN THE PREVIOUS chapters, I have tried to present my understanding of the core insights of the Pure Theory of Law and defend it. This understanding stands somewhat in contrast to most contemporary readings of the Pure Theory, according to which the Pure Theory should best be portrayed as driving a middle way between moralism and realism:[1] from moralism it takes anti-reductivism and from realism it takes separability of law and morality. According to this standard reading, the main contribution of the Pure Theory is a cross-cutting of the strengths of existing theses. According to my reading, the Pure Theory does something much more radical: it presents an entirely new approach to the problem of law.[2]

The common reading is also responsible for the analysis of certain defects in the Pure Theory. Most critical attacks levelled against the Pure Theory concur with the claim that even if we tidy up all of its versions and formulations, even if we bring together all is different doctrines and iron out their surface inconsistencies, what we are left with is a theory which on its most favourable reading carries a fundamental contradiction at its core. Even authors who, like Stanley L Paulson, can hardly be accused of being hostile to the project of the Pure Theory cannot deny that the main proponent of the Pure Theory, Hans Kelsen, is 'running off in two different directions at once'.[3] Antonio Bulygin famously referred to a fundamental 'antinomy' in Kelsen's work.[4] If we take these to be the last words on the Pure Theory, then it is hard to see how the latter could ever be more than a partially interesting political theory supported

---

[1] See SL Paulson, 'Introduction' in H Kelsen, *Introduction to the Problems of Legal Theory* (Oxford, Oxford University Press, 2002) xxvi; J Raz, 'The Purity of the Pure Theory' in S Paulson (ed), *Normativity and Norms: Critical Perspectives on Kelsenian Themes* (Oxford, Oxford University Press, 1998) 237.

[2] I have already presented the arguments in this chapter in C Kletzer, 'Absolute Positivism' (2013) 42 *Netherlands Journal of Legal Philosophy* 87.

[3] SL Paulson, 'The Weak Reading of Authority in Hans Kelsen's Pure Theory of Law' (2009) 19 *Law and Philosophy* 131, 167.

[4] E Bulygin, 'An Antinomy in Kelsen's Pure Theory of Law' (1990) 3 *Ratio Juris* 29.

by a set of applaudable political and moral convictions, or how it could ever be worthy of the serious academic engagement it actually attracts.

What is barely ever considered is the possibility that the contradiction stems not from the Pure Theory itself but from the mistaken idea that the Pure Theory tries to steer a middle way. After all, it is hard to see how one could drive a middle way between moralism and reductionism without entering a lazy compromise, without ignoring the contradiction that such a compromise necessarily involves. But what if the Pure Theory, in contrast to Hart's positivism, never attempted a middle way? Put differently, what if the Pure Theory attempted a 'middle way' between reductionism and moralism only in the way in which Kant drove a 'middle way' between rationalism and empiricism, that is, no real middle way at all? The Kantian solution to the great philosophical impasse is not conciliatory, but radical: what Kant attempted was not to reconcile two opposed world views by creating a syncretistic compromise of both, but to turn everything upside down and to submit the very possibility of us relating to the world to a fundamental reassessment. Kant introduced not a compromise, but a *Revolution der Denkungsart*, an intellectual revolution.

In this chapter, I suggest that on this very general level the Pure Theory indeed presents a fundamentally Kantian solution to the jurisprudential impasse and that when we read the Pure Theory with Kant, we can see that its heart does not lie in simply proposing a new concept of law, but rather in rethinking the possibility of us relating to the law qua possible object of knowledge and in submitting this possible relation to a revolutionary overturn. The Pure Theory approaches solving the problem of the ontology of the law ('What is law?') by translating it into a new, 'transcendental', epistemology ('How can we relate to the law qua possible object of knowledge and how do we have to conceive of a law to which we can actually relate?'). It turns out that the implicit everyday epistemology of our relation to the law, even though held dear by common sense, is actually incoherent and impossible, and ultimately has to be jettisoned.

Even though such a radically Kantian approach to the Pure Theory is hardly new or revolutionary, not much has been made of it so far, with the greatest intellectual effort being spent on the previously devised un-Kantian model of the middle way, even though this model is neither very intellectually challenging nor promises many chances of success.

The present reading starts with the assumption that the Pure Theory can only hope to be successful if it does not try to steer a middle way between reductionism and moralism but instead tries to overcome the opposition by making clear that both opponents of the opposition rest on the same ill-conceived convictions about legal validity. Both take it that the law cannot be normative from itself. In this, natural law theory and reductionism agree.

By correcting this conviction, the Pure Theory does not present a middle way between the suppositious opponents, but rather presents a true alternative to a spurious alternative; it does not present a third way, but an actual second way.

So the Pure Theory's insight starts with the demonstration that moralism and reductionism are both half-truths, which cannot simply be added together or mixed up in order to get a full truth. Rather, the Pure Theory shows, quite in line with the Kantian resolution of the antinomy, that both theses are expressions of the same mistake, expressions of the same erroneous approach to the law: both take the law to be derivative of something else.

In contrast to this, the Pure Theory tries to find a new approach to the understanding of the law, an approach that takes seriously the constitutive functions of the law. It tries to understand the validity of the law as resting in the law itself. As such, it is an attempt to find a philosophically satisfactory formulation of absolute positivism.

II. RELATIVE POSITIVISM

Defining positivism has itself become part of heated academic disputes. However, since we have to start somewhere, we are going to identify positivism with one of the following theses:

(R_1) In any legal system, whether a given norm is legally valid does not depend on its merits.[5]

(R_2) The validity and the content of the positive law cannot be derived from moral premises.

In this form, positivism presents itself as a negative or relative position, ie as the rejection of certain normative relations of derivation. Positivism, understood in this way, first and foremost tells us what the law is not. We will call this kind of positivism 'negative', or 'relative positivism'.[6]

---

[5] Gardner's definition runs: '(LP) In any legal system, whether a given norm is legally valid, and hence whether it forms part of the law of that system, depends on its sources, not its merits.' However, he also claims that '"source" is to be read broadly such that any intelligible argument for the validity of a norm counts as source-based if it is not merit based'. Gardner takes the two categories source and merit to be 'jointly exhaustive of the possible conditions of validity of any norm'. However curious such a claim or stipulation may be, it does allow us to omit as redundant the sources element from the definition of positivism. See J Gardner. 'Legal Positivism: 5 1/2 Myths,' (2001) 46 *The American Journal of Jurisprudence* 199.

[6] For an instructive typology and historical discussion of positivism and its schools, see B Bix, 'Legal Positivism' in MP Golding and WA Edmundson (eds), *Blackwell Guide to the Philosophy of Law and Legal Theory* (London, Blackwell, 2005) 29.

III. ABSOLUTE POSITIVISM PROJECTED

However, the question is not only what the law is not. It is also what the law is. Now, a provisional definition of absolute positivism emerges when we try to answer this positive question without abandoning our commitment to relative positivism. What would such an answer look like? What would we be left with if we retained our commitment that the law's content is not dependent on moral merit? All that we would be left with to base the validity and content of the law on would be *the law itself*. Usually, if we ask for the basis of something, we would expect it to be something else. If the answer to a question asking what is the basis of X is X itself, then the answer could as well be: X is based on nothing or on nothing else. A theory that tries to base the validity of the law on the law itself or on nothing, which is the same, could be called positive, or absolute positivism:

(A₁)   In any legal system, whether a given norm is legally valid depends entirely on the law.

Or

(A₂)   The validity and the content of the positive law is based on the law itself or on nothing, which is the same.

This sounds like a terribly dialectical and mysterious claim. However, all we have done here is to make explicit what is already present in R_1 and R_2: to claim that the law is source based means that the law is based on law, which means that the law is based on nothing. In its content, absolute positivism is thus no more radical than relative positivism. One cannot be committed to relative positivism and not already be committed to absolute positivism, and if one finds absolute positivism unpalatable as an idea, one better finds a way to give up relative positivism. The advantage of relative positivism, if it can be considered an advantage at all, is that it does not immediately give away the radicalness of the claim it is making. Much of contemporary positivism seems to be wedded to relative positivism for exactly this reason. Contemporary positivism's main claim is that all law is 'source based'. This sounds sober enough. But what does it mean? Since, in this context, 'source' can only mean 'legal source', all that the claim that the law is source based can mean is that the law is law based or that the law is, in an important respect, baseless, which is the same.

   Note also that the above formulation of absolute positivism is just a projection or extrapolation of this concept derived from relative positivism. It is just a working concept, the naming of a theoretical place which we can imagine yet know little of. The concept of absolute positivism will be developed below.

One way to avoid insight into the radicalness of positivism is to divorce questions about the criteria of membership from questions about the criteria of the authority or bindingness of the law. Such a move is meant to delegate all quirky questions of normativity to a theory different from the sources thesis and to thus take explanatory pressure off the latter. However, it is hard to see how this could solve rather than exacerbate the problem, because: (i) divorcing the two questions simply adds another pressing question to an already pressing one; (ii) by divorcing the question of normativity from the question of membership, one has admitted that the normativity of the law cannot be a function of the law qua law, but that it has to come from somewhere else, be it from a comprehensive moral theory (Finnis) or teleological relations to right reasons (Raz); by doing this, however, one has admitted that the real theoretical weight is lifted by that other theory and that the law just plays a certain role in what is fundamentally a moral theory;[7] this unwittingly turns positivism from a comprehensive legal theory into an accidental element of a moral theory; and (iii) finally, in however manner the problem of bindingness is ultimately thought to be solved (and I share Kelsen's view that it cannot be solved separately from the question of membership), it still leaves the problem of the baselessness of the criteria of membership unsolved.

In contrast to this, the Pure Theory is at least partially an attempt to make philosophical sense of absolute positivism and to face the challenges of common sense.

As its title suggests, the Pure Theory demands purity. This means that it deals with the positive law and the positive law alone. Thus, it cannot consider any principles beyond the law, and accordingly has to answer the question of the validity of the law from the law itself. In this attempt to perform the seemingly impossible lies the essence of the Pure Theory, and in this attempt it is more programme than completed doctrine.

Of course, at first sight, a programme to base the validity of the law on the law itself must seem ridiculous. How should the law ever be able to ground and constitute itself? What could this even mean?

---

[7] See P Soper, 'Some Natural Confusions about Natural Law' (2002) 90 *Michigan Law Review* 2393. I do not think that Raz's practical difference thesis, ie the claim that in order to be authoritative the law has to purport to make a practical difference by excluding or pre-empting appeal to dependent reasons, which include first-order moral reasons, gets us very far here, since the question whether the law actually makes a practical difference has to be decided by moral reasons. See J Raz, *The Authority of Law* (Oxford, Clarendon Press, 1979) ch 3. See also S Shapiro, 'The Difference That Rules Make' in B Bix (ed), *Analyzing Law: New Essays in Legal Theory* (Oxford, Clarendon Press, 1998) 39; J Coleman, 'Incorporationism, Conventionality, and the Practical Difference Thesis' (1998) 4 *Legal Theory* 381.

IV. AGRIPPA'S TRILEMMA

The Pure Theory answers this question indirectly, via the detour of a sceptical argument about the derivation of validity in general. This is because it is not only absolute positivism that struggles with the derivation of validity. Indeed, when trying to account for legal validity, relative positivism faces problems of its own kind, problems which, when attended closely, turn out not to be mere obstacles, but impossibilities of a principled kind.

Relative positivism faces the following well known, but still fundamental, problem: assuming that no legal norm is valid in itself, that no legal norm is valid because of its content but has to be posited in order to be valid, then each legal norm depends in its validity on another legal norm, since being posited means being lawfully posited, which in turn means being posited according to a valid legal norm. Now, if the validity of every legal norm necessarily depends on the validity on another legal norm, we can demonstrate, in line with the classic pyrrhonic argument, that there can exist no valid legal norms at all, since the resulting chain of derivations of validity leads to the following trilemma:[8] we get one of (i) a dogmatic acceptance of certain truths, ie the abandonment of derivation as such, (ii) an infinite regress or (iii) a logical circle.

Option (i) does not even attempt to present a solution to the problem, but is simply an abandonment of the premise, ie of the universal need for derivation, or, in our case, the abandonment of the universal positivity of the law. Any legal norm can be justified by claiming that certain norms are valid in and from themselves.

According to (ii), however, no legal norm at all can be valid: an infinite regress means that a final justification cannot be reached and thus no norm is thoroughly justified.

Finally, option (iii), again allows any legal norm to be valid, since every possible legal norm can be derived from a logical circle.

The trilemma shows us that with logical necessity the premise of positivism, ie the requirement of legal norms to be based on other legal norms, leads to the situation in which either no law or any possible law can be valid. Put differently: if there is to be valid law, then anything is law, otherwise nothing can be law.

Now, contemporary positivism is but a formulation of this paradox. It primarily consists in moving about the horns of the trilemma and in trying to combine circularity and dogmatism, ie to combine the methods of validating any law with the method of validating no law in such a way that the specific validity of the law can be explained. Contemporary positivism finds its most

---

[8] H Albert, *Traktat über kritische Vernunft* (Tübingen, JCB Mohr, 1991) 15.

comprehensive formulation in the so-called sources thesis, which states that the question of whether a legal norm is legally valid depends on the sources of this legal norm and not on its moral merit.[9] With that, however, we have before us less of a theory of law and more of the formulation of a problem, namely the aforementioned trilemma: how can a norm meaningfully derive its validity from a source which itself must derive validity from another source without leading to either an infinite regress or a circularity, or giving up the requirement of derivation?

The situation is quite clear in Hart and has been discussed many times. Hart takes the regress as finding its end in the rule of recognition.[10] In order to escape dogmatism, ie in order not to link the capacity of the rule of recognition to end the regress to some special intrinsic quality of the rule of recognition, in some element of its content, he says that the rule of recognition is a rule which is accepted by the organs of the given legal community.[11] Thereby, however, he has escaped dogmatism only at the cost of accepting circularity:[12] the rule of recognition depends in its validity on the acceptance by organs, the character of which in turn depends on legal norms, the validity of which can be traced to the rule of recognition.[13]

With such a circle, everything can be justified: I can, for instance, set up the state of Egopolis, a legal system the rule of recognition of which states that everything I declare to be law immediately becomes law. In my legislative function I then declare myself to be the only organ of the state of Egopolis and in my function as that organ I accept the rule of recognition. Then I posit further legal norms. The validity of these legal norms can be traced to a rule of recognition, which is valid since it is accepted by the organs of the legal order, ie by me. Thus, everything I declare to be law is valid law.

---

[9] '(LP) In any legal system, whether a given norm is legally valid, and hence whether it forms part of the law of that system, depends on its sources, not its merits.' Gardner (n 5) 199.

[10] HLA Hart, *The Concept of Law*, 2nd edn (Oxford, Oxford University Press, 1994) 94.

[11] ibid 114.

[12] For a recent discussion of this circularity and attempts at its solution, see B Tamanaha, 'Socio-Legal Positivism and a General Jurisprudence' (2001) 21 *OJLS* 1; K Culver and M Guidice, *Legality's Border* (Oxford, Oxford University Press, 2010).

[13] One might be tempted to think that Kelsen and Hart here deal with different questions: whereas Hart's rule of recognition mainly offers a solution to the problem of membership, ie the question of which norms belong to a legal order, Kelsen's basic norm wants to answer the question of validity, which in his view also includes the question of the binding nature of norms. Hart does, of course, also tackle the problem of validity and bindingness. The main difference is that, in contrast to Kelsen, it makes sense to Hart to look at membership in isolation, ie from a purely external point of view, whereas for Kelsen it is pointless to think about membership without also considering validity. What matters for the present discussion, however, is that both do actually deal with both questions and the difference can be disregarded at this stage. See CS Nino, 'Some Confusions Surrounding Kelsen's Concept of Validity' in Paulson (n 1) 253–61.

In order to escape the arbitrariness of the grounding of validity in such circles, Hart introduced a further condition of validity: it is not enough for the rule of recognition to be accepted by the organs; the norms flowing from it also have to be by and large obeyed by the subjects, ie the legal order has to be effective.[14] This is not the case in the above-outlined state of Egopolis. It might thus seem that the problem of circularity, and thus the problem of the validity of arbitrary norms, is solved.

Unfortunately, it is not. Hart solved the problem of circularity by introducing a condition which is not itself legally justified and which thus can only apply dogmatically: from within the myriad of rules of recognition which can be legitimised by a circular argument, this one shall be valid, and is actually obeyed by the subjects. Put differently: for each legal order that is actually obeyed, a circular argument can be found which legitimises the rule of recognition. Thus, as a circular argument, the rule of recognition simply provides legitimacy to any given effective legal order—or, to be precise, it provides the semblance of legitimacy. In truth, the normativity shall not be conditioned by the rule of recognition itself, but by the effectivity of the legal order. The century-old question of how normativity can be derived from effectivity, of how validity can be derived from obedience, is not solved but, rather, is obscured by conjuring up the circular argument.[15]

Hart does not solve the problem of the specific validity of the positive law, but he veils it by switching between circularity and dogmatism in order to escape an infinite regress.

Theories that add moral elements, like Dworkin's interpretivism or Finnis's natural law theory, at least in the respect discussed here, do not fare much better. Rather, the problem of justification of validity of the law is part obfuscated, part exacerbated by the addition of moral norms, which are themselves in want of justification. They just add another layer of complexity to the problem without taking it head on.

Now, the trilemma argument does not simply state that it is problematic or difficult to find validity in chains of derivation, but it demonstrates that it is logically impossible to derive validity at all. Note the strengths of the claim:

---

[14] Hart (n 10) 117.

[15] For a discussion of this issue, see A Marmor, 'Legal Conventionalism' (1998) 4 *Legal Theory* 509; G Postema, 'Coordination and Convention at the Foundations of Law,' (1982) 11 *OJLS* 165. For attempt to find a solution via efficacy see G Postema, 'Conformity, Custom, and Congruence: Rethinking the Efficacy of Law' in MH Kramer, C Grant, B Colburn and A Hatzistavrou (eds), *The Legacy of HLA Hart: Legal, Political, and Moral Philosophy* (Oxford, Oxford University Press, 2008) 46.

derivation of validity is *logically* impossible. This is the only truly absolute result that relative positivism can provide.

Now, the curious twist of absolute positivism and the Pure Theory is that its own constitution of validity is based on this logical impossibility. It is, so to speak, only in the transit through absolute scepticism about validity that the necessity of absolute positivism becomes clear. Whereas modern Anglo-American positivism despairs over the logical acuteness of this scepticism, the Pure Theory, in so far as it is an attempt to find a formulation of absolute positivism, takes the strictness of this sceptical insight as its origin. The truth of relative positivism lies in the insight that there can be no validity when one hopes to derive validity, when one wants find validity in an external relation of one norm to another. It is easy to see that the only way to overcome relative positivism and the ensuing absolute impossibility of deriving validity is to let go of the attempt to find the validity of one norm in an external relation it has to another norm. But how is this to be done?

V. ABSOLUTE POSITIVISM DEVELOPED

The argument runs parallel to the overcoming of Agrippa's trilemma in epistemological debates about the impossibility of justification in general: after all, Agrippa's trilemma applies not only to the derivation of validity, but to any form of derivation. In the broader context of justification in general, the sceptical trilemmatic argument claims that no belief can ever be justified. This is so because any belief can only be justified by another belief, which also has to be justified in order to justify the first. This set-up, however, invariably leads to the known trilemma: we must (i) accept that the chain of justifications goes on forever (infinite regress); (ii) believe that there is a certain kind of belief that is capable of justifying other beliefs without itself being justified (dogmatism); or (iii) think that certain beliefs can either directly or indirectly justify themselves (circularity). What is the way out? The classical Kantian way out of this trilemmatic structure has been to attend closely to how exactly the trilemma emerges and which commitments it presupposes, and then to give up or reverse those commitments. This leads to a rethinking of how we conceive of 'a relation' in general. This is done by attending to what is negated in all three sceptical arguments and to reconstruct from this a true form of rationality:

> What is negated in all three arguments of the trilemma of justification is the nativeness and independence of the *relation*. To the ontological bias of our realist common sense the relation is but the empty and variable space between the actual things, between the substances, between the empirically given entities. In contrast to this

thing-ontological dogmatism, scepticism correctly draws from all this the conclusion, that our cognition of the actual existing things is variable and fundamentally empty.[16]

As long as we stick to our realist common sense, ie the idea that what is actual are the things in isolation and that the relation between these things is only contingent, secondary and external to them, then we should not be surprised that our relation to these things also turns out to be contingent and ultimately external to these things. It is thus our realist ontological commitments, tacitly implicit in our common sense, which lead to the epistemological impasse of the impossibility of justifying any belief about the world. Consequently, it is in the name of having a working epistemology, ie in the name of being able to know anything at all, that we have to criticise, rethink and ultimately change our ontological commitments. Ultimately, this means that we have to take the relation to be the actually existing entity and the 'thing' to be the secondary entity. This is what the Kantian reformulation of the object from being a 'thing in itself' to being a 'phenomenon' or a 'thing for us', which is the same, actually means.[17]

Now, in facing the trilemma, jurisprudence has to demand that juristic common sense go through a similar critique and ultimately throw out its implicit ontological commitments: it demands a reversal of the conviction that the relation is secondary and external to the *relata* to the conviction that the relation is fundamental and primary.

What does this mean?[18] Relative positivism takes the law to be a sum, an aggregate, of legal norms, the interrelation of which is external to these legal norms. Its fundamental thesis, the sources thesis, states that a norm derives its validity from another positive norm—though derived it must be. Absolute positivism, in contrast, starts with the insight that the impossibility of establishing legal validity by means of derivation stems from the separation of the law into a legal norm, on the one hand, and the grounding of validity, on the other. Absolute positivism, in contrast, accepts that the law is not a sum of legal norms which are then, successively, somehow related to each other, but rather that the positive law itself *is* a legal relation. The law is not a collection of norms, but the interrelation between these norms, ie it is the creation, justification and application of norms. To say that the positive law is actually legal relation is simply to say that the law *is* legal process.

---

[16] KW Zeidler, *Grundriß Der Transzendentalen Logik* (Cuxhaven, Traude Junghans Verlag, 1997) 149. Original emphasis.

[17] See H Allison, *Kant's Transcendental Idealism. An Interpretation and Defence* (New Haven, Yale University Press, 1983) 29.

[18] For some reasons why the transcendental argument looks slightly different in the legal context than it does in the context of theoretical philosophy, see C Kletzer, 'Kelsen, Sander, and the Gegenstandsproblem of Legal Science' (2011) 12 *German Law Journal* 785.

VI. LAW AS LEGAL PROCESS

To illustrate this seemingly puzzling claim that the law *is* legal process (namely the process of legally determining the lawful use of force), it is helpful to have a brief look at a crucial exchange between Merkl,[19] Verdross[20] and Kelsen.[21]

The issue of contention between the three authors was the following: given that the law sets out conditions of legality, who is competent to determine whether these conditions have been met? Is common reason and, by extension, legal science[22] called upon to make that decision? Or is it the law itself via a legal organ that has to decide this case?

Merkl claimed that for a legal organ to act legally, ie for it to act as a legal organ, it has to act in accordance with the authorising norm and thus it has to act within certain limits. Whether or not it has indeed acted within these limits determines whether or not the act actually is a legal act or not. This is thus crucial question. But who decides this? Take the case of a show Parliament in a theatre performance enacting a show statute, or the case where the actual Parliament of Australia acts clearly outside the competence conferred upon it by the constitution—say, it threatened to punish jaywalkers in Norway with the death penalty. In both cases, we would have legal non-acts. It seems clear that everyone capable of the rudimentary use of reason is called upon to make that call. However, Kelsen and his student Sander[23] claimed that since to decide whether an act is a legal act is a legal rather than an empirical question, and thus itself requires a legal act, only legal officials can make this decision.

---

[19] A Merkl, 'Das Recht im Lichte seiner Anwendung' in HR Klecatsky et al (eds), *Die Wiener rechtstheoretische Schule. Schriften von Hans Kelsen, Adolf Merkl, Alfred Verdross* (Vienna, Verlag Österreich, 2010) 955; A Merkl, 'Das doppelte Rechtsantlitz' in Klecatsky et al (ibid) 893; A Merkl, 'Die Lehre von der Rechtskraft' in Klecatsky et al (ibid).

[20] A Verdross, 'Eine Antinomie der Rechtslehre' in Klecatsky et al (ibid) 1123.

[21] H Kelsen, 'Was ist ein Rechtsakt?' in Klecatsky et al (ibid) 1129.

[22] Since the idea that 'legal science' is possible is a speciality of Continental legal thought, and since in the anglophone world the idea of legal science always appears slightly silly, I do not rely on any strong notion of legal science in order to make the argument in this chapter. Legal science here is the placeholder for any fully rational and systematic treatment of the law and is the full development of common reason. This important difference between Continental and anglophone legal thought has to do with the reception of Roman law on the Continent and the relative lack of such a reception in the common law. The reception of Roman law meant that the law was learned and taught at universities, which were founded mainly for the purpose of studying old sources of Roman law, by legal scholars, whereas the common law was learned and taught where it happened as law, ie at the courts, by legal practitioners. R Scheuermann, *Einflüsse der historischen Rechtsschule auf die oberstrichterliche gemeinrechtliche Zivilrechtspraxis bis zum Jahre 1861* (Berlin, DeGruyter, 1972) 43. See also F Wieacker, *A History of Private Law in Europe: With Particular Reference to Germany*. Tony Weir trans. (Oxford, Clarendon, 1996).

[23] For a discussion of the troubled but intellectually exciting relation between Kelsen and Sander, see C Kletzer, 'Fritz Sander' in R Walter et al (eds), *Der Kreis um Hans Kelsen. Die Anfangsjahre der Reinen Rechtslehre* (Vienna, Manz, 2008) 445–70.

Merkl had a powerful rejoinder: the law contains rules about which organ can act in certain cases and also how it can act. Now, according to Merkl, it would be absurd to require a legal decision for settling which organ can act: if a self-proclaimed 'judge' on Speakers' Corner were to convict the Prime Minister of treason, everybody, and not just a legal organ, is competent to decide that we are not dealing with a legal act here. Otherwise, it seems, every private person, simply by pretending to issue a legal act, would make it necessary for a true legal act to declare this pretentious legal act to be a non-legal act. It seems that this absurd result can be avoided only by giving everybody's common reason and thus ultimately legal science a competence to preselect which acts are to be considered to even count as candidates for legal acts in the first place. But why, Merkl claims, should a case where a non-official acts be treated differently from a case where an otherwise competent organ acts clearly outside the competence conferred upon it by the law? After all, both act without competence.

Verdross summarises Merkl's position as follows:

> It is not immediately clear why, given that the question of who should be the legislator is determined by reference to the constitution, we should not also be allowed to check by reference to the constitution and 'availing ourselves of common reason' whether the legislator has been following the 'ways' of legislation predetermined by the constitution. And the same question has to be asked when we, 'seen through the eyes of common reason' establish an 'error of law' or an 'error of fact' of a judge.[24]

The dilemma is the following: either we take only the law itself to be competent to determine what counts as law, whereupon it seems that nothing can be excluded *ex ante* from being law, or we accept that legal science determines whether a legal official has acted within the limits set out by the higher norm, whereupon we seem to be accepting that legal science and not the law is the ultimate arbiter and thus also the ultimate source of legal validity.

Verdross calls this an antinomy of jurisprudence and proposes a third, rather Hartian in content, solution: he suggests that it is neither inner-legal criteria nor criteria of legal science that solve the issue of determining what is law, but rather extra-juristic criteria of legal sociology. Verdross asks us to imagine the following situation: a couple of men gather and act like the chamber of a supreme court. Now, this situation can have at least three meanings:

> It could be (a) harmless jest, (b) a criminally liable assumption of authority or (c) the successful instalment of a revolutionary organ. One only needs to think of the revolutionary establishment of the workers and military councils close to the end of WWI.[25]

---

[24] Verdross (n 20) 1124.
[25] ibid 1126–27.

The point Verdross is trying to make is that one cannot tell *ab initio* which of the three options legally is the case. Rather, this only transpires as a sociological and ultimately historical fact later on.

> We are here thus not dealing with acts that can *ab initio* and merely on the basis of the legal order be qualified as official acts, but rather with acts which only subsequently take on the quality of official acts. This is possible since they constitute the conditions for further stages in the legal process, eg that the decisions of these persons is then enforced by the executive organs. Such a qualification, however, cannot be made by means of a legal science looking only at the legal order, but it has to derive from a social science looking at the actual social reality.[26]

This seems like an attractive solution. However, according to Kelsen (and Sander), it is untenable. In order to show why this is the case, Kelsen argues that we have to separate two questions. The first is: 'What is a legal act?' This question must be answered by something other than the law itself, ie by legal science and ultimately jurisprudence.

> The Pure Theory of Law defines the concept of a legal act as an act via which a legal norm is posited or applied; and it claims that an act can only be an act creating or applying law if it corresponds to the norms which which within the legal order regulate the creation and application of law, ie when the act is posited on the basis of the legal order.[27]

This is uncontroversial, and both Merkl and Verdross accept it and base their claims on it. The second question, however, is the following: 'How are we to decide whether an act which subjectively presents itself as a legal act actually is one objectively?' If this question were merely a question of logical subsumption, ie if the logic employed by legal science were capable of giving us a single definite answer to this question, then legal science could indeed determine this question. However, subsumption, Kelsen argues, gives us not one solution, but a set of possibilities. In order to come to a conclusion, what is thus needed is not inference, but decision, not thinking, but willing. Now, although science is competent to infer, it is not competent to decide. The decision therefore has to be done by the law itself.

> After all, the specifically juridic problem whether a given act is a legal act, is not a question relating only to juridic subsumption. What matters here is a *decision*, an authentic, constitutive, legally binding decision, to which the legal order attaches specific legal consequences. Such a decision is not a mere function of reason, but of the will; and thus neither legal science nor any other science can make this decision.

---

[26] ibid 1127.
[27] H Kelsen, 'Was ist ein Rechtsakt?' in HR Klecatsky et al (eds), *Die Wiener rechtstheoretische Schule. Schriften von Hans Kelsen, Adolf Merkl, Alfred Verdross* (Vienna, Verlag Österreich, 2010) 1130.

> To make a legally binding decision means to posit an (individual) norm. Legal science as a science cannot produce any norms.[28]

Anybody can have opinions about the law, about the limits of legal competence or about the legality of certain legal acts, and these opinions can certainly be more or less good or reasonable opinions—it is, however, only the law itself that settles the case, that establishes which opinion is legally correct.

So, whether or not an organ has acted *ultra vires*, ie outside of the conditions set down by the legal order for its actions, has to be decided by the law. To see that this is a necessary result, one only has to ask the following question: what makes an act a legal act? It is not some intrinsic quality, but the fact that it has legal consequences. But how are those legal consequences determined? Legal consequences are fully determined not by the legal act itself (A_1) or *in abstracto* by the authorising norm, but by another legal act (A_2) that sets down the consequences (eg execution of a claim) of A_1. Thus, whether A_1 is indeed a legal act has to be settled by A_2 in a preliminary question.

This is no different than in the case of the relevance of facts. Facts do not decide cases by themselves as naked legal facts, or facts-in-themselves, but do so in so far as they are established as facts in the legal process, in so far as they are facts-for-the-law. This establishment of facts also happens as an authoritative settlement of preliminary questions. Since facts are relevant to the law only as legally established facts, the legal establishment of facts is thus unavoidable.

This has often been lamented as an unfortunate formalism or even relativism of the law: even if everyone knows that it is the case that X (OJ Simpson has killed Nicole Brown Simpson and Ron Goldman), the law says that it is not the case that X (it is not the case that OJ Simpson has killed Nicole Brown Simpson and Ron Goldman). But this functioning of the law is less a sign of entrenched relativism than a logical necessity mirroring quite straightforward Kantian insights: the law cannot possibly be concerned with facts as they are in themselves, independently from the law. This is not a demand, but a logical necessity. The law can in principle only deal with facts as they appear to the law. Within those appearances, it has to single out certain facts as established. There is no other way the law could possible act. Even if it tried to be as much in line as possible with the common view of facts and even if it were to tie the establishment of the legal facts to the common view[29] by, say, making general surveys the basis of the establishment of legal facts, this would still be just a way of establishing legal facts. There would still not be any immediate access to the facts as they are in themselves; rather, the survey would now be the way the facts appear to the law. Just as for our knowledge things in themselves

---

[28] ibid 1131.
[29] This is, of course, what the law tries by means of the jury system.

(ie non-experienceable things) are off limits and thus have to be irrelevant also in our theory of knowledge, so too for the legal process facts-in-themselves (ie non-establishable facts) are off limits and have to be irrelevant both to the law and in our theory of law. If our theory of law needs to make reference to objects to which the law in principle cannot make reference, then this has to be a fatal defect in our theory. This insight is thus in no way a precursor to relativism. Rather, conversely, it is the only way to save the law from relativism.

Why is this relevant? It is relevant because, just as the question of whether a fact is a legal fact needs to be established in a preliminary question of a legal act, so the question of whether an act is a legal act has to be established in a preliminary question of another legal act that sets down the legal consequences of the first legal act. What is true for the establishment of facts is also true for the establishment of legal acts.

> It is not the legal act as such to which the legal consequences (eg execution) attach, but the establishment of the legal act. If the conditioning fact for a legal consequence is a legal act, then always and under all circumstances the existence of this legal act has to be established in a legal process, ie by a legal organ and it has to be decided whether the act is question is a legal act, ie whether it is actually just the act to which the legal order attaches the consequence.[30]

This, however, means that each legal act has to implicitly, in a preliminary question, posit the legal character of all acts of which the legal act in question is a consequence. A legal act executing a court judgment thus has to determine and confirm in a preliminary question that the court judgment it executes was actually a legal act, which implicitly involves the determination that the Act of Parliament creating the statute on which the court judgment is based was a legal act, which in turn implicitly involves determining that the creation of the constitution on which the Act of Parliament was based was a legal act. This, of course, cannot be done without, as the Pure Theory calls it, 'presupposing the basic norm': the creation of the historically first constitution can only be considered and affirmed as a legal act if a norm is presupposed that turns this factual occurrence of trying to create a constitution into a legal act of actually creating a constitution. So the basic norm is not an academic gimmick, but a legal reality implicitly referred to and relied upon in every legal act. In this sense, every legal act and thus the law as such 'is sovereign'. It is thus not the case that the basic norm creates the law, which then simply 'exists'. This is a common but fundamentally misguided image. Rather, the existence of the law is always precarious since it is in each and every legal act that the law constantly has to create itself: in the legal act, the legal organ legally establishes that the conditions of its own legality are given, which can only work by

---

[30] Kelsen (n 27) 1132.

presupposing the legal existence of a certain first constitution. The law thus has to be constantly sustained, established and re-established in the legal process, which confirms the legal nature of legal acts and which thus confirms the law as law. The law is not established once and for all in the basic norm and from then on we have the law; rather, it has to constantly self-referentially keep itself in existence by claiming to be in existence.

All of this, however, also means that an implicit authority to review other legal acts can never be excluded. So, even when there is a chain of appeals, and even if it is the supreme court that ultimately decides something, each lower court and each officer has to, as a preliminary question, have already answered the question whether the decision of the supreme court actually is a legal act.

> Since the appeals procedure necessarily has to be limited, the appeal has to lead to an act of last instance which is not open to further examination in *this specific* procedure and which is thus typically found to to possess final legal force. However, insofar as the legal order attaches legal consequences to such an act which has acquired final legal force—and this is always the case since the act is posited only for the purpose of its consequences—then this act has to be examined in a subsequent legal procedure and its legal character has to be authentically established.[31]

In this sense, even a policeman applying a court order has to have decided, and thus has to be competent to decide, whether the court order is valid law. But in order to do that, he has to have decided, and thus has to be competent to decide, that the statute on which this order is based and the constitution on which the statute is based are valid law. This is less puzzling than it might sound. The law is kept in existence by applying it as law. This is what I have identified as the effectiveness of law in chapter three. If one policeman were to annul the creation of the first constitution by not accepting it as legally binding in the preliminary question of his informal procedure of whether or not to apply a court order, then he himself might face legal consequences by officers who do not come to the same conclusion as he does about the first constitution. However, if more and more officers came to that conclusion and if the law flowing from this specific constitution were no longer generally applied, then it would indeed be difficult to still consider it to be the law. Rather, we would have witnessed a revolutionary change. It is difficult to see how a theory that takes the law to exist independently of its application by everyone could explain such a revolutionary change. The law is thus not the existence of rules, but more of a swarm of such sovereign decisions.

Verdross's own example is very instructive here. Verdross argued that in the case of the decision of the chamber of a self-appointed supreme court, we do not know in advance whether this is actually a legal act, since this depends on

---

[31] Kelsen (n 27) 1134. Original emphasis.

subsequent facts. Kelsen accepts this, reinterprets it and extends it to all law: the validation of legal acts in subsequent legal acts is not a paradoxical quirk of a counter-example, but lies within the nature of legal acts per se, which do not have the nature of being legal acts in themselves, but only in being legal acts for other legal acts. Retrospective validity is not an anomaly of some legal phenomenon, but a feature of the law per se. Such retrospective validation cannot be effected by social science, but has to be done by the law itself.

> The difference between legal and social science is not to be found in the fact that only social science but not legal science has human behaviour as its object. The difference is rather to be found in the fact that legal science has human behaviour as its object only insofar as this human behaviour is determined to be a condition or consequence of legal norms, whereas social science relates to actual human behaviour insofar as it is determined causally, ie insofar as it is determined as cause and effect.[32]

This does, however, solve the trilemma: the trilemma emerges because we try to take the legal act as existing independently of its relations to other legal acts, because we, on the one hand, believe the legal act to have its nature in itself but, on the other hand, claim that it's legal nature is derived from another legal act. The trilemma is defused as soon as we see that legal acts do not have their nature of being legal acts in themselves, but only in being legal acts for other legal acts.

To claim that the law is legal process means that the problem of the validity of a legal norm is not a philosophical or jurisprudential problem but a legal one, to be solved not by legal theory but by the law itself.[33] For absolute positivism, validity is not to be determined by legal theory, but by positive law itself.[34] One is tempted to adduce the unlikely support of Dworkin here, who claimed that jurisprudence was the general part of adjudication, ie that the task which we believe is to be fulfilled by legal philosophy is actually always already fulfilled by the law itself.[35]

---

[32] Kelsen (n 27) 1139.

[33] This is not Raz's point, that legal propositions are internal to a legal discourse and do not make sense outside of such a discourse, or Hart's point, that questions about what 'legally' ought to happen only makes sense relative to a discourse constituted by the rule of recognition. It is not about a discourse at all. It is a claim about the actual legal process, ie about what legislators, judges, legal officials and, ultimately, legal subjects do and how an interpretation of these actions is schematised by legal rules.

[34] Nino's helpful distinction between 'rules' and 'judgements of validity', leading to two different chains of derivation, takes the latter 'judgements of validity' to be 'typically formulated by jurists'. With 'jurists', he presumably has academics in mind. The authentic and thus truly relevant 'judgments of validity', however, happen not in an academic but in a legal context in the legal process itself, ie as judgements (in Nino's sense) done by parliamentarians (judging that the constitution is valid), by judges (judging statutes and constitutions to be valid), by executive forces (judging court orders, statutes and constitutions to be valid) and by legal subjects (judging executive commands, court orders, statutes and constitutions to be valid). See Nino (n 13) 257.

[35] 'Jurisprudence is the general part of adjudication, silent prologue to any decision in law': R Dworkin, *Law's Empire* (Cambridge, MA, Harvard University Press, 1986) 90.

Absolute positivism thus solves the problem of the validity of law by declaring that this problem has already been solved by the law itself.[36]

In identifying validity as a problem to be solved by legal theory, relative positivism implicitly claims a final competence in relation to the determination of legal validity. It is unaware that in doing so it actually arrogates a legal competence—a competence, however, which is at odds with its own doctrine of the positivity of the law. In relative positivism, positivism thus recoils back at itself: the argument rightfully directed at natural law theory, ie that one must not confuse philosophical content with legal content and that the moral philosopher does not have competence to posit laws, also cuts against relative positivism.

Relative positivism is thus only a semi-positivism, a half-hearted doctrine that is always exposed to a *tu quoque* claim.

Absolute positivism, in contrast, makes the precarious attempt not to overstep the limits of its competences when talking about the positive law. After all, that there are competences which are conferred by positive law and which can be overstepped is the fundamental positivistic insight. Absolute positivism thus does not try to establish the validity of the law, as this cannot be done without giving up the fundamental positivistic convictions. Rather, it lets the law be, it lets it be valid, its lets the mode of validity immanent in the law be itself. It thus defers all competence to the law itself.

---

[36] In the context of Bruno Celano's theory of validity as disquotation, this means that we have to locate the activity of disquotation in the positive law itself. By 'disquotation', the following is meant: just as in a minimalist theory of truth, the trivial criterion of truth can be given as '"*p*" is true iff *p*' or '"Snow is white" is true iff snow is white', which allows one to disquote sentences, to use a sentence which was formerly only mentioned, to make *p* out of '*p*'. In Celano's disquotational theory of validity a similar relation applies: 'the norm "*q*" is valid iff *q*' or 'The norm "Children ought to obey their parents" is valid iff children ought to obey their parent'. Now, Celano thinks that the disquotational statements are statements of meta-jurisprudence, and that 'validity' is a device in the vocabulary of 'a substantive ethical theory purporting to specify the conditions under which the law, or particular legal norms, ought to be obeyed' (235), ie it belongs to the vocabulary of an inquiry into what the law ought to be and 'not to the vocabulary of a scientific description of positive law as it actually is. This latter is, however, precisely the use to which validity as disquotation has been put, in the Pure Theory of Law, by Kelsen himself. In the Pure Theory of Law, a conceptual, necessary relation holds between positive law, on the one hand, and validity (validity as disquotation) on the other hand: positive legal norms are, as such, binding' (236). Conversely, in Kelsen's work, the concept of disquotation features as a technique not of meta-ethics or legal science, but of the positive law itself. For Kelsen, positive legal norms 'as such' can never be binding, since positive legal norms 'as such,' ie irrespective of their relation to other legal norms, separated from the legal process, are not positive legal norms. In contrast to what Celano writes, Kelsen's criterion of binding force is this: '"*p*" has binding force, if another norm *q* as a scheme of interpretation allows interpreting it as having binding force'. Or '*p*' has binding force if another norm *q* disquotes '*p*'. See B Celano 'Validity as Disquotation' [1999] *Analisi e diritto* 35.

VII. THE BASIC NORM

This deferral of the problem of validity of the law to the law itself finds its legal expression in the basic norm.[37] The basic norm marks the borderline between law and legal theory. As we have seen above, the positive law, if it wants to be valid as positive law, must not depend in its validity on conditions given to it by legal theory, but has to posit the conditions of validity for itself. It does precisely this in presupposing (German *voraus-setzen*, or pre-positing) the conditions of validity in the basic norm.[38]

The law presupposes the basic norm. Now, since Kelsen has written that we can presuppose the basic norm but do not have to,[39] one might be under the impression that the presupposition of the basic norm is a psychological act. In fact, it is not a psychological act but a logical relation. It is not the case that one first has to presuppose the basic norm in order to then say something about the law. Rather, one has always already presupposed the basic norm by, for instance, questioning the validity of a putative legal norm, as questioning the validity of a legal norm means asking if, amongst the other valid legal norms, there is one that authorises the creation of the norm in question. In asking this question, one has already presupposed the validity of other norms and thus the validity of the basic norm. One cannot ask a legal question, one cannot say or think anything legal, without already having presupposed the basic norm. Presupposing the basic norm thus is not a psychological accident but is, by logical necessity, implied in speaking about the law.[40] The law presupposes its own validity. It is thus the law and not we that presupposes the basic norm, and in presupposing the basic norm the positive law posits itself.

As we have seen in chapter three, the basic norm is simply the statement that law is law; it is thus just the restatement as a norm of the theory of law presented here, ie that 'the use of force is to be applied according to the law'. As such, it is not a mysterious entity arbitrarily placed at the top of the legal hierarchy, but is a necessary element of a sober examination of the law.

---

[37] 'The basic norm *is* a judgment of validity', yet at the same time 'this fundamental judgement of validity, according to Kelsen, is itself a norm'. Nino (n 13) 258.

[38] 'Auch das Voraussetzen ist ein Setzen, aber ein Setzen, das das Setzen zugleich als aufgehoben setzt' ['Presupposing, too, is a positing. It is a positing, however, which posits its own positing as cancelled']: D Henrich, *Hegel im Kontext* (Frankfurt am Main, Suhrkamp, 2010) 120.

[39] See H Kelsen, *Reine Rechtslehre*, 2nd edn (Vienna, Verlag Österreich, 2000) 224.

[40] See U Bindreiter, 'Presupposing the Basic Norm' (2001) 14 *Ratio Juris* 143, 168: 'It seems that the presupposition of the basic norm was intended, by Kelsen, to evoke a specifically "legal" use of language. Since the linguistic form of norm-formulations (used to issue norms) and of norm-statements (used to "describe" norms) may well be exactly the same, the difference between norm-formulation and norm-statement must lie in the illocutionary force of the respective utterances.'

One can, of course, avoid presupposing the basic norm. However, one can only do so by not speaking or thinking about the law as law. Thus, the presupposition of the basic norm is more an academic problem and less a legal one.

The presupposition of the basic norm brings us into the internal space of the law. In the presupposition of the basic norm, the law tells us what is law and what are legally relevant facts. Viewed from the inside, there is no reality outside of the law that is independent of the law yet relevant to it.

Because of this, philosophy has nothing to tell the law which the law would not know from itself. If there is to be law, then law exists by necessity. Put differently: viewed from the point of view of the law, the law exists necessarily and the validity of the law leaves open no meaningful questions to be answered by legal philosophy. Viewed from the point of view of philosophy, however, there can be no positive law and no legal validity. Relative positivism is simply the law viewed from the point of view of philosophy. The irresolvable paradox relative positivismfaces is that for it, there can be no valid law at all.

It is thus the positive law itself that has fulfilled and completed a task which philosophy set itself and which it necessarily failed to complete, since a law that is in need of a constitution through philosophy cannot be positive law. Relative positivism is a philosophical doctrine which thinks it is a doctrine about the law but is actually a doctrine about its own, ie philosophy's, supreme competence, a doctrine, however, which conflicts with its own positivistic commitments. As a theory of the supreme competence of philosophy and reason, relative positivism is actually closer to a natural law theory than it might at first appear. Whereas relative positivism takes reason and its mouthpiece philosophy to be the final arbiter of all formal questions relating to the law, natural law theory takes reason and its mouthpiece philosophy to be the final arbiter of *all* questions relating to the law. In relation to natural law, relative positivism has given up some competences over the positive law. Absolute positivism surrenders *all* competences over the positive law.

Absolute positivism this is a philosophical doctrine about the limits of philosophy. As a philosophical doctrine about the limits and incompetence of philosophy, absolute positivism to a certain extent has to be both reflexive and anti-philosophical.[41] In this sense, the anti-intellectualism and anti-philosophical stance entrenched in the classic British common law

---

[41] The reflexive nature of positivism comes to light as an inner dividedness of positivism. Positivism was always torn between a philosophical and a decidedly anti-philosophical strand. A throughout philosophical positivism is a more recent phenomenon and positivistic tradition is rife with strong anti-philosophical tendencies. There is, for instance, the common opinion that the philosophical reflection of the law relates to the positive law as institutes to pandects, ie as a textbook introduction to the real law. Philosophy can help write textbooks for novices. However, it cannot help us master the complexity of the positive law itself. See FC von Savigny, *Vom Beruf unserer Zeit für Gesetzgebung und Rechtswissenschaft* (Hildesheim, Georg Olms, 1967) 115.

tradition is not only a national fancy, but also a necessary expression of a fully positivistic approach to the law.

A true positivism thus has to be able to bear these anti-philosophical tendencies within it. Positivism cannot be itself without at the same time being a doctrine about the end of philosophy, about the outpouring of philosophy into the world. In so far as the loss of God has meant that philosophy was promoted from the maidservant, the *ancilla*, to the vicar of theology, we can say that only an absolute positivism can free itself from a mode of thinking that was formed by the paradigms of theology. This is because the problem with the loss of God is not only that we lose the firm foundations of the divine rules and the secular rules based on these divine rules; it is also that the loss of God has changed the paradigm of the validity of rules itself. Without God, rules hold and apply differently, they are valid in a different manner and sense. And whereas relative positivism secretly awaits the revelation of a final validity, this is, it awaits and lacks the absolute, absolute positivism has learned the full lesson of the absolute immanence of validity: the world does not lack legitimacy. Neither does the law.[42]

In this chapter, I have tried to present the Pure Theory as a way to formulate an absolutely positivistic theory of law. In so doing, I moved the analysis away from the middle way and towards an understanding of the Pure Theory as a philosophical grappling with the radical self-constitution of legal validity.

However, since the Pure Theory not only attempts to deal with legal validity but also tries to present a programme of legal scientific work, and since absolute positivism with its anti-philosophical tendency is an unpopular position, the proposed reading of it is precarious. It is, however, both promising and much needed, since it defends the Pure Theory against the charge of inconsistency and tries to formulate a coherent idea of the Pure Theory.

---

[42] H Blumenberg, *Die Legitimität der Neuzeit* (Frankfurt am Main, Suhrkamp, 1999). See also C Kletzer, 'Kelsen and Blumenberg: the Legitimacy of the Modern Age' (2014) 25 *King's Law Journal* 19.

8

Conclusion

In this book, I have tried to demonstrate that we gain a better understanding of the law if we view it as an order of force or violence.

The driving force behind this approach has been the conviction that if we get the basic set-up wrong we end up chasing our own tail in the attempt to make sense of the law.

The view that the law is not just a collection of demands or standards but an order of force is a view that is shared both by the most common and pedestrian understanding of the law and by the most sophisticated or even esoteric traditions in the history of philosophy. It is only a certain kind of mid-level and, I feel, half-baked intellectualism that is keen to deny this. The law enjoys a degree of actuality or realness that is lacking in other, only seemingly similar, enterprises, like morality. Everybody who has ever encountered the law in its operation as law knows that it is not just words. This realness of the law is, I feel, often willingly lost in contemporary jurisprudential seminaries, where the debate turns successively flimsy.

This is a defect which I think the Pure Theory has always avoided. It resists the excessive sanitisation of the law, which I fear we are witnessing in much of contemporary jurisprudence. The Pure Theory has achieved analytic clarity without being tempted to give up its realism.

At the core of the Pure Theory's inquiry is the question of how violence or force can be ordered. It is easy to see how affairs in the world can be ordered by force. But how is force or violence itself ordered? How can force itself be affected? I think this question is the crux of a truly philosophical theory of law. Whilst the world can be ordered by force, force itself cannot be ordered by force. Put differently: we cannot understand how force is ordered if we suppose that it is itself ordered by force because we cannot understand how the ordering force is itself ordered. If it is not force that allows us to order force, what remains? After all, the law is in the business of ordering force and it is quite successful in that business. How can we understand this? The attractive proposal of the Pure Theory of Law has been to suggest and develop the idea that it is only interpretation or language that can order force.

This is possible only because 'an order' is something that is both out there in the world and inside our heads. Language creates order by picking out an order from the many possible orders out there in the world and the law (as language) orders force and violence by picking out certain forms of force or violence as lawful. This understanding allows us to understand both how the law is real (how it actually orders force) and how it is also normative (how it sets standards).

If the law is understood as a collection of demands, then it remains purely 'in the books', insulated from the world, and we need to outsource the problem of the realness or actuality of the law to dubious theories of coercion, enforcement and motivation. It then remains mysterious to see how the law transcends the realm of words into actuality, and much intellectual effort is spent to chasing this chimera. The law does, of course, stand with one foot in the books, but we have to get its true relation to the world right to see how it can stand with the other firmly in the world and thus see how it towers over both.

Giambattista Vico called the law 'una severa poesia',[1] a severe poetry. The severity of the law is not confined to the fact that it uses drastic language and sometimes gory ideas; rather, its entire relation to the world is itself severe. Why severe? Both 'describing' and 'demanding' are in a sense unsevere, as they keep to themselves and do not immediately change the world. The law, conversely, immediately intervenes in the world. Its severity or brutality lies, as I have tried to show, in its peculiar mix of describing and demanding, ie in describing the world not as it is but as it is demanded to be.

This, as I hope to have shown, solves many of the classic puzzles of jurisprudence in a both elegant and comprehensive manner. It provides explanations of the specific normativity of the law, of its positivity, of its relation to morality and of its relation to the world of facts all emanating from one unitary understanding or view of the law. As such, I think it is not only worth considering as a possible alternative to the common model of understanding the law, but it presents a standpoint superior to the ones currently swaying the jurisprudential community.

---

[1] G Vico, *The New Science of Giambattista Vico*, trans TG Bergin and MH Fisch (Ithaca, Cornell University Press, 1948) 350.

Bibliography

Albert, H, *Traktat über kritische Vernunft* (Tübingen: J.C.B. Mohr, 1991).

Alexy, R, 'Some Reflections on the Ideal Dimension of Law and on the Legal Philosophy of John Finnis' (2013) 58 *American Journal of Jurisprudence* 97.

Allison, H, *Kant's Transcendental Idealism: An Interpretation and Defence* (Yale: Yale University Press, 1983).

Anscombe, GEM, 'Modern Moral Philosophy' (1958) 33 *Philosophy* 1.

Apel, KO, *Understanding and Explanation. A Transcendental-Pragmatic Perspective*, G Warnke trans (Cambridge, MA: MIT Press, 1984).

Arendt, H, *The Life of the Mind* (San Diego: Harvest, 1978).

Atria, F, 'Games and the Law: Two Models of Institution', in (1999) 85 *Archiv für Rechts- und Sozialphilosophie* 309–347.

Banham, G, *Kant's Transcendental Imagination* (London: Palgrave Macmillan 2005).

Bates, B, Greif, A and Singh, S, 'Organizing Violence' in (2002) 46 *Journal of Conflict Resolution* 599–628.

Bayles, MD, 'A Concept of Coercion,' in Pennock and Chapman (eds), *Nomos XIV: Coercion* (Chicago: Aldine-Atherton, 1972) 16–29.

Beltrán, JF and Ratti, GB (eds), *The Logic of Legal Requirements. Essays on Defeasibility* (Oxford: Oxford University Press, 2012).

Bernstorff, J von, *The Public International Law Theory of Hans Kelsen: Believing in Universal Law* (Cambridge: CUP, 2010).

Betti, E, 'La "vindicatio" romana primitiva', (1915) 39 *II Filangieri* 321–44.

Bejczy, I, 'Tolerantia: A Medieval Concept' in (1997) 58 *Journal of the History of Ideas* 365–384.

Bindreiter, U, 'Presupposing the Basic Norm,' (2001) 14 *Ratio Juris* 143–75.

Bix, B, 'Legal Positivism' in MP Golding and WA Edmundson (eds), *Blackwell Guide to the Philosophy of Law and Legal Theory* (London: Blackwell, 2005).

Blackburn, S, *Essays in Quasi-Realism* (Oxford: OUP, 1993).

Blumenberg, H, *Die Legitimität der Neuzeit* (Frankfurt am Main: Suhrkamp, 1999).

Bobbio, N, 'Law and Force', in (1965) 49 *The Monist* 321–41, 321.

Bobbio, N, 'Norma', in *Enciclopedia Einaudi, Volume 9* (Torino: Einaudi, 1980) 891–2.

Bonafé, BI,' International Law in Domestic and Supranational Settings' in J Kammerhofer et al (eds), *International Legal Positivism in a Post-Modern World* (Cambridge: CUP, 2014).

Brundage, A, 'Prostitution in Medieval Canon Law' in V Bullough and A Brundage (eds), *Sexual Practices and the Medieval Church* (Buffalo: Prometheus Books, 1982), 149–60.

Brunner, H and Schwerin, CF von, *Deutsche Rechtsgeschichte. Band II* 2nd edn (Berlin: Duncker und Humboldt, 1928).

Bulygin, E, 'Permissive norms and normative systems', in A Martino and F Socci-Natali (eds), *Automated Analysis of Legal Texts* (Amsterdam: Elsevier Science, 1986) 216.

Bulygin, E, 'An Antinomy in Kelsen's Pure Theory of Law' (1990) 3 *Ratio Juris* 29–45.

Celano, B, 'Validity As Disquotation,' (1999) *Analisi e diritto* 35–77.

Coady, CAJ, 'The Moral Reality in Realism' (2005) 22 *Journal of Applied Philosophy* 121.

Coleman, J, 'Incorporationism, Conventionality, and the Practical Difference Thesis' (1998) 4 *Legal Theory* 381.

Crawford, J, *Chance, Order, Change: The Course of International Law, General Course on Public International Law* (Leiden: Brill 2014).

Culver, K and Guidice, M, *Legality's border* (Oxford: OUP, 2010).

Del Mar, M et al (eds), *Legal Fictions in Theory and Practice* (Cham: Springer, 2015).

Dostoyevsky, F, *The Brothers Karamazov*, (London: Penguin, 2003).

Dworkin, R, *Law's Empire* (Cambridge, MA: Harvard University Press, 1986).

Dworkin, R, 'Hart's Posthumous reply', (2017) 130 *Harvard Law Review* 2096.

Dyzenhaus, D, *Legality and Legitimacy. Carl Schmitt, H Kelsen, and Hermann Heller in Weimar* (Oxford: OUP, 1997).

Ehrenberg, KM, *The Functions of Law* (Oxford: OUP, 2016).

Enoch, D, 'Giving Practical Reasons' (2011) 11 *The Philosopher's Imprint* 1–22.

Enoch, D, 'Reason-Giving and the Law' in L Green et al (eds), *Oxford Studies in the Philosophy of Law, vol. 1* (Oxford: OUP, 2011), 1–38.

Fichte, JG, *Foundations of Natural Right*, Neuhouser trans (Cambridge: CUP, 2000).

Finnis, J, *Natural Law and Natural Rights*, 2nd ed (Oxford: OUP, 2011).

Finnis, J, 'Law as Fact and as Reason for Action: A Response to Robert Alexy on Law's "Ideal Dimension"' (2014) 59 *American Journal of Jurisprudence* 85.

Frankfurt, H, 'Coercion and Moral Responsibility,' in *The Importance of What We Care About* (New York: Cambridge University Press, 1988) 65–86.

Gadamer, HG, 'Text and Interpretation' in DF Michelfelder and RE Palmer (eds), *Dialogue and Deconstruction: The Gadamer-Derrida Encounter* (Albany: State University of New York Press, 1989).

Galston, WA, 'On the Alleged Right to Do Wrong: A Response to Waldron' (1983) 93 *Ethics* 320.

Gardner, J, 'Legal Positivism: 5 1/2 Myths,' (2001) 46 *The American Journal of Jurisprudence* 199–227.

Gardner, J, 'Law as a Leap of Faith' in *Law as a Leap of Faith: Essays on Law in General* (Oxford: OUP, 2012) 1–18.

Geach, PT 'Assertion' (1965) 74 *The Philosophical Review* 449–465.

Gell-Mann, M, *The Quark and the Jaguar: Adventures in the Simple and the Complex* (New York: Henry Holt, 1994).

Green, L, 'Introduction' in HLA Hart, *The Concept of Law*, 3rd ed (Oxford: OUP, 2012) xv–lv.

Gunderson, M, 'Threats and Coercion' (1979) 9 *Canadian Journal of Philosophy* 247–259.

Hage, J, 'The deontic furniture of the world' in J Stelmach et al (eds), *The Many Faces Of Normativity* (Kraków: Copernicus Center, 2013) 73–114.

Hage, J, 'Separating Rules from Normativity' in Michal Araszkiewicz et al (eds), *Problems of Normativity, Rules and Rule-Following*, (Cham: Springer, 2015), 13–30.

Harris, JW, 'Kelsen's Concept of Authority' (1977) 36 *CLJ* 353.

Hart, HLA, *Essays on Bentham. Jurisprudence and Political Theory* (Oxford: OUP, 1982).

Hart, HLA, 'Kelsen's Doctrine of the Unity of Law' in HLA Hart, *Essays in Jurisprudence and Philosophy* (Oxford: Clarendon Press, 1983) 309;

Hart, HLA and Honoré, AM, *Causation in the Law*, 2nd ed (Oxford: OUP, 1985).

Hart, HLA, *The Concept of Law*, 2nd ed (Oxford: OUP, 1994).

Hart, HLA, 'Kelsen Visited', in Bonnie Litschewski Paulson and Stanley L. Paulson (eds), *Normativity and Norms. Critical Perspectives on Kelsenian Themes* (Oxford: OUP, 1998).

Hathaway, OA and Shapiro, SJ, 'Outcasting: Enforcement in Domestic and International Law.' (2011) *Faculty Scholarship Series. Paper* 3850. http://digitalcommons. law.yale.edu/fss_papers/3850.

Heathwood, C, 'Monism and Pluralism about Value' in I Hirose and others (eds), *The Oxford Handbook of Value Theory* (Oxford: OUP, 2015).

Hegel, GWF, *Elements of the Philosophy of Right*, Nisbet trans (Cambridge: CUP, 1991).

Henrich, D, *Hegel im Kontext* (Frankfurt am Main: Suhrkamp, 2010).

Herstein, O, 'Defending the Right To Do Wrong' (2012) *Cornell Law Faculty Publications*, Paper 339.

Heusler, A, *Das Strafrecht der Isländersagas*, (Leipzig: Salzwasser, 1911).

Hindriks, F, 'Constitutive Rules, Language, and Ontology' in (2009) 71 *Erkenntnis* 253–275.

Jarvis Thomson, J, 'Normativity' in R Shafer-Landau (ed), *Oxford Studies in Metaethics*, vol 2 (Oxford: OUP, 2007).

Kant, I, 'Kant on the Metaphysics of Morals: Vigilantius's Lecture Notes,' in P Heath and JB Schneewind (eds), *The Cambridge Edition of the Works of Immanuel Kant. Lectures on Ethics* (Cambridge, 1997).

Kant, I, *The Critique of Pure Reason* (Cambridge: CUP, 1999).

Kelsen, H, *Das Problem der Souveränität und die Theorie dies Völkerrechts-Beitrag zu einer reinen Rechtslehre* (Vienna: JC Mohr, 1920).

Kelsen, H, *Der soziologische und der juristische Staatsbegriff. Kritische Untersuchung des Verhältnisses von Staat und Recht* (Wien: Deuticke 1928).

Kelsen, H, *Die philosophischen Grundlagen der Naturrechtslehre und des Rechtspositivismus* (Berlin: Heise, 1928).

Kelsen, H, *Reine Rechtslehre: Einleitung in die rechtswissenschaftliche Problematik* (Vienna: Deuticke, 1934).

Kelsen, H, *General Theory of Law and State* (Cambridge, MA: Harvard University Press, 1949).

Kelsen, H, *Pure Theory of Law*, 2nd ed, Knight trans (Berkeley: University of California Press, 1967).

Kelsen, H, 'The Idea of Natural Law' in Hans Kelsen, *Essays in Legal and Moral Philosophy*, O Weinberger (ed), P Heath (trans) (Dordrecht: Reidel, 1973), 27–60.

Kelsen, H, *General Theory of Norms* (Oxford: Clarendon Press, 1991).

Kelsen, H, *Introduction to the Problems of Legal Theory. A Translation of the First Edition of the Reine Rechtslehre or Pure Theory of Law*, BL Paulson and S Plaulson trans (Oxford: Clarendon Press, 2002).

Kelsen, H, 'Was ist ein Rechtsakt?' in HR Klecatsky et al (eds), *Die Wiener rechtstheoretische Schule. Schriften von Hans Kelsen, Adolf Merkl, Alfred Verdross* (Vienna: Verlag Österreich, 2010), 1129.

Klecatsky, HR, et al (eds), *Die Wiener rechtstheoretische Schule. Schriften von Hans Kelsen, Adolf Merkl, Alfred Verdross* (Vienna: Verlag Österreich, 2010).

Kletzer, C, 'Kelsen's development of the Fehlerkalkül-Theory' in (2005) 18 *Ratio Juris* 46–63.

Kletzer, C, 'Custom and positivity: an examination of the philosophic ground of the Hegel–Savigny controversy' in A Perreau-Saussine and J Murphy (eds), *The nature of customary law: philosophical, historical and legal perspectives* (Cambridge: CUP, 2007).

Kletzer, C, 'Fritz Sander' in *Der Kreis um Hans Kelsen. Die Anfangsjahre der Reinen Rechtslehre* Robert Walter (et al) eds (Wien: Manz, 2008), 445–470.

Kletzer, C, 'Kelsen, Sander, and the Gegenstandsproblem of Legal Science,' *German Law Journal* 12 (2011): 785–810.

Kletzer, C, 'Absolute Positivism' in (2013) 42 *Netherlands Journal of Legal Philosophy* 87–99.

Kletzer, C, 'Kelsen and Blumenberg: the Legitimacy of the Modern Age', in (2014) 25 *King's Law Journal* 19–33.

Kletzer, C, 'The Normative Jinx' in (2017) *OJLS* gqx010. doi:10.1093/ojls/gqx010.

Kramer, M, *In Defence of Legal Positivism. Law Without Trimmings* (Oxford: OUP, 1999).

Kramer, M, 'On the Moral Status of the Rule of Law' in (2004) 63 *CLJ* 65.

Lamond, G, 'Coercion, Threats, and the Puzzle of Blackmail' in AP Simester and ATH Smith (eds), *Harm and Culpability* (Oxford: Clarendon Press, 1996) 215–238.

Lamond, G, 'The Coerciveness of Law' (2000) 20 *OJLS* 39–62.

Lamond, G, 'Coercion and the Nature of Law' (2001) 7 *Legal Theory* 35–57.

Lindahl, H 'Dialectic and Revolution: Confronting Kelsen and Gadamer on Legal Interpretation' in (2003) 24 *Cardozo Law Review* 769–798.

Lintott, AW, *Violence in Republican Rome* (Oxford, Clarendon, 1968).

Lippold, R, *Recht und Ordnung. Statik und Dynamik der Rechtsordnung* (Vienna: Manz, 2000).

Luzzatto, G 'Von der Selbsthilfe zum römischen Prozess' (1956) 73 *Zeitschrift der Savigny-Stiftung für Rechtsgeschichte: Romanistische Abteilung* 29–67.

MacCormick, N, 'Norms, Institutions, and Institutional Facts' in (1998) 17 *Law and Philosophy* 301–345.

MacCormick, N, *Institutions of Law. An Essay in Legal Theory* (Oxford: OUP, 2007).

Marmor, A, 'Legal Conventionalism' (1998) 4 *Legal Theory* 509.

Marmor, A, *Interpretation and Legal Theory* (Oxford: Hart, 2005).

Marmor, A, *Philosophy of Law* (Princeton: Princeton University Press, 2011).

McBride, NJ, and Steel, S, *Great Debates in Jurisprudence* (Palgrave Macmillan 2014.

Merkl, A, *Die Lehre von der Rechtskraft: Entwickelt aus dem Rechtsbegriff. Eine rechtstheoretische Untersuchung* (Wien: Deuticke 1923).

Merkl, A, 'Das doppelte Rechtsantlitz' in Hans R. Klecatsky et al (eds), Die Wiener rechtstheoretische Schule. Schriften von Hans Kelsen, Adolf Merkl, Alfred Verdross (Vienna: Verlag Österreich, 2010), 893.

Merkl, A, 'Das Recht im Lichte seiner Anwendung' in Hans R. Klecatsky et al (eds), *Die Wiener rechtstheoretische Schule. Schriften von Hans Kelsen, Adolf Merkl, Alfred Verdross* (Vienna: Verlag Österreich, 2010), 955.

Merkl, A, 'Die Lehre von der Rechtskraft' in Hans R. Klecatsky et al (eds), *Die Wiener rechtstheoretische Schule. Schriften von Hans Kelsen, Adolf Merkl, Alfred Verdross* (Vienna: Verlag Österreich, 2010).

Murray, MJ and Dudrick, DF, 'Are Coerced Acts Free?' (1995) 32 *American Philosophical Quarterly*, 118–123.

Mousourakis, G, *A Legal History of Rome* (London: Routledge, 2007).

Nagel, T, *Mortal Questions* (Cambridge, CUP 1979).

Nieburg, HL, 'Uses of Violence', in (1963) 7 *Journal of Conflict Resolution* 43–54.

Nino, CS, 'Some Confusions Surrounding Kelsen's Concept of Validity' in SL Paulson and B Litschewski-Paulson (eds), *Normativity and Norms: Critical Perspectives on Kelsenian Themes* (Oxford: OUP, 1998) 253.

Noë, A 'Is the World a Grand Illusion?' in A Noë (ed), *Is the Visual World a Grand Illusion?* (Thorverton: Imprint Academic, 2002).

Nozick, R, 'Coercion,' in S Morgenbesser, P Suppes, and MG White (eds), *Philosophy, Science, and Method: Essays in Honor of Ernest Nagel*, (New York: St. Martin's Press, 1969) 440–72.

Oberdiek, H, 'The Role of Sanctions and Coercion in Understanding Law and Legal Systems' in (1976) 21 *American Journal of Jurisprudence* 71.

Oliver, P, *Legal Fictions in Practice and Legal Science* (Rotterdam: Rotterdam University Press, 1975).

Paulson, S, 'Material and Formal Authorisation in Kelsen's Pure Theory' (1980) 39 *CLJ* 172.

Paulson, SL, 'An Empowerment Theory of Legal Norms' in (1988) 1 *Ratio Juris* 58.

Paulson, SL 'Introduction' in Hans Kelsen, *Introduction to the Problems of Legal Theory* (Oxford, OUP, 2002).

Paulson, SL, 'The Weak Reading of Authority in Hans Kelsen's Pure Theory of Law' in (2009) 19 *Law and Philosophy* 131–171.

Pennock, JR and Chapman, JW (eds), *Nomos XIV: Coercion* (Chicago: Aldine-Atherton, 1972).

Postema, G, 'Coordination and Convention at the Foundations of Law,' (1982) 11 *OJLS* 165.

Postema, G, 'Conformity, Custom, and Congruence: Rethinking the Efficacy of Law,' in MH Kramer, C Grant, B Colburn and A Hatzistavrou (eds), *The Legacy of H.L.A. Hart: Legal, Political, and Moral Philosophy* (Oxford: OUP, 2008), 46.

Raz, J, *The Authority of Law* (Oxford: Clarendon Press, 1979).

Raz, J, 'Hart on Moral Rights And Legal Duties' (1984) 4 *OJLS* 123–131.

Raz, J, 'Authority, Law, and Morality' in J Raz, *Ethics in the Public Domain: Essays in the Morality of Law and Politics* (Oxford, OUP 1995).

Raz, J, *The Concept Of a Legal System. An Introduction to the Theory of Legal System* (Oxford: Clarendon, 1997).

Raz, J, 'The Purity of the Pure Theory' in Stanley Paulson (ed), *Normativity and Norms: Critical Perspectives on Kelsenian Themes* (Oxford: OUP, 1998) 237.

Raz, J, *Practical Reason and Norms* (Oxford: OUP, 1999).

Raz, J, *Between Authority and Interpretation. On the Theory of Law and Practical Reason* (Oxford: OUP, 2009).

Rehfeldt, B, 'Die Vergeistigung des Rechtes. Zur Frage der Gesetzmäßigkeiten der Rechtsentwicklung' (1950) 67 *Zeitschrift der Savigny-Stiftung für Rechtsgeschichte. Germanische Abteilung* 373.

Rehfeldt, B, 'Recht, Religion und Moral bei den frühen Germanen' (1954) 71 *Zeitschrift der Savigny-Stiftung für Rechtsgeschichte. Germanische Abteilung* 10, 7–8.

Ripstein, A, 'Authority and Coercion' (2004) 32 *Philosophy and Public Affairs* 2–35.

Rodriguez-Blanco, V, 'Reasons in Action v. Triggering Reasons: A Reply to Enoch on Reason-Giving and Legal Normativity' in 7 *Problema* 2013, at biblio.juridicas.unam.mx/revista/Filoso aDerecho.

Sangiovanni, A, 'The Irrelevance of Coercion, Imposition, and Framing to Distributive Justice' in (2012) 40 *Philosophy and Public Affairs* 79–110.

Savigny, FC von, *System des heutigen Römischen Rechts* (Berlin: Veit, 1840).

Savigny, FC von, *Vom Beruf unserer Zeit für Gesetzgebung und Rechtswissenschaft* (Hildesheim: Georg Olms, 1967).

Schauer, F, *The Force of Law* (Cambridge, MA: Harvard University Press, 2015).

Schauer, F, 'On the Nature of the Nature of Law' in (2012) 98 *Archiv für Rechts- und Sozialphilosophie* 457.

Scheuermann, R, *Einflüsse der historischen Rechtsschule auf die oberstrichterliche gemeinrechtliche Zivilrechtspraxis bis zum Jahre 1861* (Berlin: DeGruyter, 1972).

Searle, JR, *Speech Acts. An Essay in the Philosophy of Language* (Cambridge: CUP, 1969).

Searle, JR, *The Construction of Social Reality* (London: Penguin 1995).

Searle, JR, *Making the Social World. The Structure of Human Civilization* (Oxford: OUP, 2010).

Sellars, W, *Kant's Transcendental Metaphysics: Sellar's Cassirer Lectures Notes and Other Essays* (Atascadero: Ridgeview, 2002).

Shapiro, S, 'The Difference That Rules Make' in Brian Bix (ed), *Analyzing Law: New Essays in Legal Theory* (Oxford: Clarendon Press, 1998), 39.

Shapiro, SJ, *Legality* (Cambridge, MA: Harvard University Press, 2011).

Simmonds, N, 'Straightforwardly False: The Collapse of Kramer's Positivism' in (2004) 63 *CLJ* 98–131.

Simmonds, N, 'Freedom, Law, and Naked Violence: A Reply to Kramer' in (2009) 59 *The University of Toronto Law Journal* 381–404.

Somek, A, 'Idealisation, de-politicization and economic due process: System transition in the European Union' in Bogdan Iancu (ed) *The law/politics distinction in contemporary public law adjudication* (Utrecht: Eleven International, 2009).

Soper, P, 'Some Natural Confusions About Natural Law,' (2002) 90 *Michigan Law Review* 2393–2423.

Sorensen, R, *Thought Experiments* (Oxford: OUP, 1998).

Spinoza, B De, 'Political Treatise', in *Spinoza, Complete Works*, Samuel Shirley trans (Cambridge: Hackett, 2002), 676–754.

Spinoza, B De, *Theological-Political Treatise*, M Silverthrone and J Israel trans (Cambridge: CUP, 2007).

Starke, JG, 'Monism and Dualism in the Theory of International Law' (1936) 17 BYBIL 74.

Staszków, M '"Vim dicere" im altrömischen Prozeß' in (1963) 80 *Zeitschrift der Savigny-Stiftung für Rechtsgeschichte: Romanistische Abteilung* 83–108.

Strauss, L, 'Jerusalem and Athens: Some Introductory Reflections' in (1967) 43 *Commentary* 43.

Tamanaha, B, 'Socio-Legal Positivism and a General Jurisprudence,' (2001) 21 *OJLS* 1–32.

Tierney, B, 'Permissive Natural Law and Property: Gratian to Kant' in (2001) 62 *Journal of the History of Ideas* 381–399.

Verdross, A, 'Eine Antinomie der Rechtslehre' in n Hans R. Klecatsky et al (eds), *Die Wiener rechtstheoretische Schule. Schriften von Hans Kelsen, Adolf Merkl, Alfred Verdross* (Vienna: Verlag Österreich, 2010), 1123.

Vico, G, *The New Science of Giambattista Vico*, translated from the third edition (1744) by Thomas Goddard Bergin and Max Harold Fisch (Ithaca: Cornell University Press 1948).

Vinx, L, *Kelsen's Pure Theory of Law. Legality and Legitimacy* (Oxford: OUP, 2007).

Vinx, L, 'Austin, Kelsen, and the Model of Sovereignty: Notes on the History of Modern Legal Positivism' in M Freeman and P Mindus (eds), *The Legacy of John Austin's Jurisprudence* (Cham: Springer, 2012) 51–71.

Vinx, L, 'The Kelsen–Hart Debate: Hart's Critique of Kelsen's Legal Monism Reconsidered' in DAJ Telman (ed), *Hans Kelsen in America: Selective Affinities and the Mysteries of Academic Influence* (Cham: Springer, 2016) 59–83.

Waldron, J, 'A Right to Do Wrong' (1981) 92 *Ethics* 21.

Walter, R, *Der Aufbau der Rechtsordnung* (Vienna: Manz, 1974).

Walter, R, et al (eds), *Der Kreis um Hans Kelsen. Die Anfangsjahre der Reinen Rechtslehre* (Wien: Manz, 2008).

Weber, M, 'Politics as Vocation' in Tony Waters et al trans, *Weber's Rationalism and Modern Society. New Translations on Politics, Bureaucracy, and Social Stratification*, (New York: Palgrave, 2015).

Wertheimer, A, *Coercion* (Princeton: Princeton University Press, 1987).

Wieacker, F, *A History of Private Law in Europe: with particular reference to Germany.* Tony Weir trans. (Oxford: Clarendon, 1996).

Yankah, EN, 'The Force Of Law: The Role of Coercion in Legal Norms' in (2008) 42 *University of Richmond Law Review* 1195–1256.

Zeidler, KW, *Grundriß Der Transzendentalen Logik* (Cuxhaven: Traude Junghans Verlag, 1997).

Index